SANE IN DAMASCUS

SANE IN DAMASCUS

AMNON SHARON

TRANSLATED FROM THE HEBREW BY
Jessica Setbon

gefen גפן
publishing house בית הוצאה לאור
JERUSALEM ◆ NEW YORK

Copyright © Amnon Sharon
Jerusalem 2006 / 5766

Typesetting: Jerusalem Typesetting
Cover Design: S. Kim Glassman

ISBN 9789652293671

1   3   5   7   9   8   6   4   2

Gefen Publishing House, Ltd.   Gefen Books
6 Hatzvi Street, Jerusalem 94386, Israel   600 Broadway, Lynbrook, NY 11563, USA
972-2-538-0247   516-593-1234
orders@gefenpublishing.com   orders@gefenpublishing.com

www.israelbooks.com

Printed in Israel   *Send for our free catalogue*

&

To Bella my wife
And to my kids Raviv, Dror and Lihi
For the love and patience throughout the years

&

The assistance and support of
Beit Halochem and Zahal Disabled Veterans Organization
in my rehabilitation has been invaluable

CONTENTS

צבא הגנה לישראל
המטה הכללי

ממכ״ל	אכ״א
מרכז קשר	למשיחרות
692016	טל:
מס״ד	כ״ם סבת תשל״ד
יבנ׳ 74	23

לכל מאן דבעין:

הנדון: מ/ 964508 פרדן אמנון.

1. הב״ל הוכרז כנעדר.

2. הודעה זו נכונה ליום : 23.1.74

לכבוד אורון, סגן

The official IDF letter declaring the author as missing in action

INTRODUCTION

I have always valued life above all else. Even in Syria, throughout the most dreadful tortures, I imagined I was grasping the edge of a deep chasm with my fingertips, trying to pull myself up, shouting, "I want to live, I don't want to die!" By the power of will and faith, I dragged myself out of the abyss. Despite the heavy burden of physical and emotional damage, I am still able to focus on the light at the end of the tunnel. In the lectures I give to army units, schools, and open houses, before audiences from a wide range of the population, I emphasize the difference between those who hope and those who believe. To me, hopers are pessimists, because they see the dark side, and because of their insecurity they hope for the best. Believers, on the other hand, are optimists, for they see the light and the good that can come from all evil.

In prison I learned to believe in God, in the God present in the heart of every person willing to accept Him, for God helps those who help themselves.

SONG

One night while deep asleep, I dreamed
I walked along the beach.
God walked beside me,
As we talked, delighted each.

Then, across the sky flashed scenes
From my life, peaceful and serene.
I saw two pairs of footprints
In the sand of each scene.

I noticed that in times of trouble
During my most miserable hours
Only one set of footprints appeared –
Not both of ours.

"God, You promised that if I followed Your path,
You would walk with me through good and bad.
If so, why did You leave me
When I was feeling so sad?"

"My dear child," God whispered,
"I would never let you come to harm.
That single pair of footprints in the sand
Were Mine – I carried you in My arms."

(popular legend)

DEPARTURE

Friday, Yom Kippur eve, 1973. A restrained carnival atmosphere prevailed in our neighborhood of Nahalat Yitzhak in Tel Aviv. Children rode bicycles and roller-skated. The streets were filled with people who had just left synagogue, while others strolled around, enjoying the special mood. But unlike in previous years, the traffic on the Tel Aviv–Haifa road was unusually heavy. "Each year Yom Kippur loses some of its sanctity. People are driving with no respect for the holiest day of the year," I commented to my wife Bella, although we did not keep the holiday strictly either. We fell asleep peacefully.

Shabbat, 10:00 A.M. A military truck drove through our street, and we saw others on the main road. I called the war reserves storage unit, and the secretary told me to stop asking questions and come right away.

At 10:30, Baruch, the deputy battalion commander, came by to pick me up. I said good-bye to three-year-old Raviv and to Bella, who was three months pregnant. "It's a war," she sighed, grasping her small stomach. "Nonsense," I denied. Just a few days earlier, right after Rosh Hashanah, I had been called up for a full training exercise. We had equipped and armed the tanks all night, and continued to work on them throughout the next day as well. "We left a hundred tanks ready and equipped. We'll just rev the engines, and the Syrians will run away," I promised her. Like me, she knew that we could trust the Israel Defense Forces.

In those days, people had complete faith in the IDF. The Six-Day War had proved that we were all-powerful supermen, and my battalion and I had been part of that success. Shortly before the outbreak of the Six-Day War, I completed officers' training and

1

was posted in Battalion 82 as commander of a tank platoon. During company training in the Revivim area of the Negev, we were placed on high alert for about a month until June 1967, when war broke out. Our battalion, part of the 7th Brigade under the command of Shmuel Gonen (Gorodish), conquered Rafiah and El Arish, and at the end of the battle we reached the Suez Canal. We held the line south of the canal for several months, during which I was promoted to first lieutenant and appointed company commander. The forces I led were stationed throughout the village of A-Shat and at the pier on the banks of the Suez Canal, across from the city of Suez. During the numerous exchanges of fire with the Egyptians, my tank was hit by several shells, but it withstood them courageously. At the end of the operational part of that war, we went up to the Golan Heights along with the entire brigade.

Bella seemed to be persuaded that this would be no worse, and with a light heart I went with Baruch to the bus depot in the Dan neighborhood. We made sure the brigade buses would go to the meeting point in Ramat Gan, and from there continue north on the coastal road. Traffic going both north and south was heavy: trucks, transport convoys with self-propelled cannons, communications vehicles, and a few buses with the first reserve soldiers. In the neighborhoods along the road, we could sense quiet preparation. People wearing white were forced to stop their prayers. They hurried to their homes, donned uniforms and walked with their families to the transport stations, embracing each other silently. The "Voice of Israel" station maintained radio silence.

We continued to flow along the river of vehicles to the clatter of the engines, not knowing exactly where we were going or why. At Caesarea junction we picked up an enlisted soldier, a paratrooper from Battalion 50, who told us that they had summoned him from home to his post on the Golan Heights. We found it hard to believe that war had begun. Just a few days before Rosh Hashanah, our air force had shot down thirteen Syrian MIGs in an air battle, and it was impossible that after such a blow the Syrians would attempt to start a war.

We arrived at Camp Fillon at about 2:00 P.M. Confusion reigned, beginning at the entrance to the camp, where the reserve unit vehicles had created a serious jam. Buses unloaded crowds of soldiers, and officers ran to and fro, directing traffic. I went to the shelters hoping to find my tanks prepared, just as we had left them a few days ago at the end of the induction exercise, but the shelters were empty and silent.

I saw the battalion commander, Lieutenant Colonel Uzi Mor, and he updated me: "Until yesterday, Friday, Barak Brigade (188th Armored Brigade) was spread throughout the Golan Heights with two regular battalions. Assuming that all the tanks are in working order and all team members are present, we have a maximum of seventy-five tanks. The third battalion will be joining them – a reserve battalion that hasn't yet been called up. Against us, the Syrians have a fighting force of 1500 tanks. Our second line will include reserve divisions, also not yet called up. The Syrian second line, about thirty kilometers north toward Damascus, has more than a thousand additional tanks, manned by their reservists. Our infantry posts along the Golan Heights include a regular battalion of paratroopers, some of whose soldiers are on leave for Yom Kippur. On the other side, the Syrians have a whole division of infantry. We have a few artillery batteries positioned in our territory, while the Syrians have dozens of batteries spread out and aimed against our forces."

I tried to imagine the lineup of forces, and asked myself where my tanks had disappeared to. Meanwhile, Uzi was informing me that the IDF was aware a war was about to break out, and that it was acting accordingly: "Since Friday, the air force has been on high alert. The enlisted soldiers have been ordered to return from leave. The soldiers of the regular seventh brigade that was in the south were flown to Rosh Pina, and on Friday night they took our tanks from the reserves storage unit at Fillon. All night long the brigade soldiers drove the tanks up to the Golan Heights, so that since Saturday morning about 160 of our tanks have been there. What's more, we have information that a Syrian commando unit has landed helicopters on the Hermon. But that's a problem for Golani Brigade and the paratroopers, not for us tankers."

I agreed with him. Uzi informed me that my company, C Company, would go up first to the Golan Heights. I would be the leading company commander. I would add the first soldiers that arrived to my company, even if they did not belong to it. Later, we learned that the war had broken out while we were speaking, around 2:00 P.M., both in the north and in the south. But at the time, we knew nothing about it.

"Which tanks do I take up to the Golan?" I asked Uzi, and he explained that the war reserves storage unit was now organizing them.

Soon afterward, ten Centurion tanks arrived at the shelter. Some were supposed to go down to Rehabilitation Unit D, while others had faults that the technical teams had tried to repair. One tank was missing its antenna bases, some were missing fenders, and most were missing the anti-bazooka plates (or fender skirts, plates that protect against HEAT [high explosive anti-tank] shells). There was even one tank whose engine was constantly running; we couldn't turn it off for fear we wouldn't be able to restart it. The tanks were equipped with a tiny amount of fuel, so we received an order that to conserve this precious commodity, we had to do all the equipping and arming without starting the engines. This meant we had to rely on manual systems, which saved on fuel but not on time or manpower.

The tank equipment was also incomplete. Each tank was supposed to have a set of special tools, but there were not enough to go around. We had to put together sets so that we would have at least one for each group of three tanks. After that they handed out size small tanker's overalls to us hefty reservists. Stuffing ourselves into these was an operation in and of itself, and the result was amusing, at least at first. We had to walk around bent over like gorillas, and when we stood up, they pinched in the groin. We laughed and joked over this, but later it was so uncomfortable that we had to roll down the top part of the overall, and in October in northern Israel, the nights had already begun to be chilly.

While I was organizing the tanks, I went behind the equipment storeroom and found Shlomo Tubi and Abraham Da'abul sitting and eating war rations. When I reprimanded them for avoiding their duties, Tubi looked pleadingly at me with his saucer eyes. He begged to be allowed to eat, since they had fasted all day for Yom Kippur. I let them finish their meal.

Then we heard hearty singing, and into the shelters drove two open trucks filled with bearded soldiers wearing *kippot*. They were Nahal soldiers from *yeshivot hesder*, the combined army-yeshiva program, who had come to assist us in preparing the tanks.

Around 8:00 P.M., the brigade commander, Reserve Colonel Ran Sarig, summoned me to his office, and ordered me and Uzi, the battalion commander, to take the tanks up to Nafah.

We had half an hour to arm the tanks. There were not enough HEAT shells in stock, so in each tank we put twelve HE (high explosive) shells, which were designed for soft targets such as infantry, jeeps, armored personnel carriers, and buildings. We also added four HEAT shells to my tank. Of course, one should never go to war with such quantities – only twelve shells instead of the seventy-two that a tank could hold. But I recall the soldiers saying, "We have plenty of shells. We'll shoot just one, and the noise will be enough to scare off the Syrians…" We all laughed, because we were the tankers who had known victory in the Six-Day War, and we lived with the feeling that no one could beat us.

I organized the crew members in the tanks, nine from the company and the tenth belonging to Uzi the battalion commander. We prepared to leave.

9:00 P.M. I drove my tank out of the shelter, mounted the turret and led the rest behind me. In the dark, a tank becomes a powerful monster. "Poor Syrians," I thought, "I feel really sorry for them. They don't know what's waiting for them since they forced us to desecrate the holy day of Yom Kippur."

Ijo Reinbenbach, the commander of B Company, strode toward me from the camp gate, having just arrived from home. He
was wearing an ironed uniform and carried his suitcase in hand,
as if about to leave for a pleasure trip. "See you after the war," he
called after me merrily, waving good-bye.

One of the tanks got stuck just at the camp exit, and we continued toward the Golan Heights with only nine tanks. A military
police jeep led us down the road.

"Everybody put your goggles around your necks, whether it's
dark or not!" I ordered on the two-way radio.

At that time, we used field goggles to measure the range to a
target. On the lens of the goggles was a graduated table, and we
could calculate in our heads the formula for estimating the range.
On the internal radio, I asked the gunner to give me the goggles
that were usually next to the commander's foot. To this day, I can
feel the anxious movements of the gunner's hand groping at my
feet in the dark. "Amnon, there aren't any goggles," he informed
me. The loader-signaler and the driver had not seen the goggles,
nor did the other tanks have any either. Without goggles, we were
blind; we could not pinpoint long-range targets. I informed the
war reserves storage unit, and they ordered me to stop and wait
for them to bring us goggles. I stopped the procession of tanks in
the center of Rosh Pina, facing north. On my left was the civilian
police station; on my right, a Shekem military canteen and a gas
station with a circular restaurant. The area was bustling with civil-
ians and soldiers. Everyone crowded around us, and I stood tall in
the turret, looking down on them from above. I blew kisses to the
girls and waved "V" for victory with my fingers until a patrol jeep
from the storage unit arrived. Someone threw a pair of goggles
in the direction of each tank. These goggles were also taken from
the boxes of equipment marked for refurbishing. I tied a lace from
my windbreaker to the goggles and put them around my neck.
Then we continued moving in the direction of the Bnot Ya'akov
Bridge.

The chains tore up the road. Pieces of tar flew at me, and the freezing wind bit my face. I went inside the tank, leaving only my eyes to peep out. At the gate of Mishmar Ha-Yarden, before the descent to Gadot, the *moshav* residents stood and waved to us. I went up onto the turret again, waved back at them and stuck out my thumb as if to signify, "Trust me, I'm protecting you." Across from us loomed the dark, threatening hills of the Golan, and the numerous bends in the road impeded our progress. One of the tanks lost its steering, and we continued on, now a convoy of eight tanks. For some reason, along with the clatter of the engines I began to hum the song "Ten Little Indians," which we had learned in English class in elementary school. I hoped the end of our story would be better than theirs.

Near the upper part of Beit Ha-Meches, the former French customs house, I had to switch tanks because of a malfunction in the radio system. I left Shuki, the radio technician, and took Mosh Karasenti, my tank driver, with me. Before mounting the new tank, Karasenti gave me a sandwich made of challah bread his mother had baked, and I devoured it quickly, unaware that my next meal would not be for a few days. We continued moving quickly in the direction of Nafah with seven tanks. Before the entrance to Nafah, we got onto the route leading north, in the direction of our regular posts. Raful (Raphael Eitan), the division commander, came onto the radio network and said to me, "'Gison (my code name),' stop where you are. Switch to '*tupee*' network, out."

I stopped the convoy, took out the paperwork I had received at the storage unit, and used the loader's flashlight to search for the radio procedures. Finally I found a slip of paper with a handwritten note: "Radio procedures for 179th."

"Why are you fooling around and not switching frequencies?!" Raful shouted in an aggravated tone of voice.

"I don't have the right piece of paper," I answered, trying to preserve radio security as I had been taught.

"Switch to '*tupee*' network on frequency 38.20, out!" In his impatience, he revealed the code word for the frequency of Barak Brigade.

I followed his instructions, and received a call from the deputy commander of Barak Brigade.

"Gison, how many tanks do you have with you?" he asked. Why on earth should I tell him how many tanks I had? On the radio we never mentioned the word "tanks." Instead, we called them "heavies," "big ones," or "black ones," and by no means would we give away their number. I explained to him that I was with a small group, and he ordered me to take them to "Mahaze" route. I was the only one in the whole company with a map. I opened it and used a flashlight to search for "Mahaze" route, but to no avail – there were no codes on my map. I informed the deputy brigade commander, who instructed me to get to the Tapline Road at all costs. The Tapline (Trans-Arabian Pipeline Company) was the old oil pipeline leading from Iraq to Zaharani in Lebanon.

We carefully turned around the seven remaining tanks and drove to Nafah camp. At the entrance to the Tapline Road, Uzi commanded, "Carry out preparation to fire and move along the Tapline without lights. Soon we will get the mission orders."

I duly ordered the company to carry out preparation to fire. The loader pushed a shell into the main gun tube and a cartridge belt into the coaxial machine gun, while I loaded a cartridge belt into the commander's machine gun. As I was busy with the machine gun, a round of fire burst from one of the tanks behind me and whizzed by my head. I bent down and called on the radio, "Attention, commanders! Slow down, the war hasn't started yet!" Later I learned that the machine gun in that tank had not been calibrated, so the moment they inserted a cartridge belt into it, the bullets fired on their own.

BATTLE

In total darkness, we got onto the Tapline Road in the area of Nafah-Sindiana. This road passed just a few kilometers next to the Syrian border and was quite narrow, exactly the width of a tank. On the western side of the road stood a fence, on the eastern side a ditch. The road rose and fell, and the field of vision was never greater than 110 yards (100 meters).

I led the tank convoy as I lay on the turret, scouting out the road and directing the driver. At the time, we did not know about the terrible battles that had taken place there, with dozens of soldiers wounded and killed. There were no visible signs of war in the field, so I was not worried about the Syrians. Instead, I was afraid the tank would fall off the road into the ditch, and above all I feared we would have to remove a tread in the cold, dark night without tools. Then the radio informed me that "Tzvika Force" was joining me. I spoke on the radio with Tzvika, the force commander, and as we talked I continued guiding the driver so that he would stay on the road. I anticipated that Tzvika Force would serve as reinforcements to replace the tanks we had left on the road, and that it would also support us with ammunition, of which we had none. Tzvika signaled to me using his rear telephone light. After a few hundred meters I got down from the tank onto the lower end of the road and saw "Tzvika Force" standing on the other side of the fence to the west. "Tzvika Force" was but one single tank, with no ammunition.

I attached him to my company and we continued moving – I directing my driver as I lay on the turret, and Tzvika driving with his tank parallel to me. Around us was pitch darkness and deathly silence. Only the rattle of the tanks disturbed the quiet as we slowly

9

advanced, eight giant monsters. Suddenly, I saw a ball of fire cut-
ting the blackness along the road and approaching me at lightning
speed. Before I could tell what it was, it exploded in front of my
tank. I went into the turret, ordered the staff to fire a shell at fighting range and aimed the tank gun at the target, but our shells fell
to the side. "Are you crazy?!" I screamed at the gunner, kicking at
his back. "I'm directing you toward the target and you're shooting sideways!"

"The rod that connects the gunner's sights with the tank gun is
broken, and the gun is not following the sights!" he yelled back at
me. To this day, my conscience bothers me for kicking him.

At that point, hellish fire broke out from the east. Dozens of
shells flew at us. I rotated the tank gun to the left and ordered the
company to open fire to the east. The tank behind me exploded
and caught fire. My tank was hit by a shell that caused a small fire,
but the loader got it under control and put it out. I was filled with
pride for my Centurion; it had proved itself again as it had in the
Six-Day War in 1967, the War of Attrition from 1968 to 1970, and
in many battles since. My tank had been hit five times in the past,
but it had never caught completely on fire, unlike the American
Patton tanks (M-60s), which when hit, turned immediately into
flaming torches.

With the first hits to our tanks, "Tzvika Force" turned around
and dashed toward Nafah. In the tumult of battle, the commander
of the last tank in my convoy noticed a tank racing past him. Without hesitation, he rotated his gun barrel toward the "Tzvika Force"
tank and shot an HEP shell at it at close range. Afterward, we said
cynically that if it had been a Syrian tank passing so close, he would
not have hit it with the first shell. But because it was an Israeli tank,
it was a direct hit. To Tzvika's good fortune, our shells were inef-
fective against tanks. The hit only stopped his tank and did not
kill the crew members, who escaped safely.

We continued shooting toward the east, and then…we heard
an enormous boom. My tank shook, and flames burst from my
hatch and the loader's. Black smoke rose into a sky lit with explo-

sions like flares. The Syrians were 150 meters from us, and they had infrared night vision equipment. They began to spray bursts of machine gun fire at the crewmen abandoning their tanks. A sharp smell of scorched earth and fire filled the air. Deathly cries came from the crew. "Abandon!" I screamed, trying to raise my voice above the earsplitting explosions.

My Centurion had betrayed me. The myth exploded, and now it stood charred like a stick of wood pulled from a fire.

My loader, Abraham Da'abul, jumped from the tank, and gunner Shlomo Tubi shouted for me to get him out – he was burning up! I bent inside and stretched out my arms. The gunner was ablaze like a torch, and I grabbed him and pulled him out. We stood on the turret engulfed in flames, open to the Syrian machine gun fire. A spray of bullets hit me in the helmet, while shots sliced into Tubi's body, killing him in my arms. I jumped down, opened the driver's hatch shelf and dragged out Moshe Karasenti, the driver, who was also aflame. The two of us rolled in a mound of dirt, extinguishing the flames that seized our overalls.

I left Karasenti and ran toward the second tank in the convoy, but it too had gone up in flames. I intended to climb onto the third tank, but then I heard another powerful boom, and a Syrian armor-penetrating shell hit that tank and it began to burn. Machine gun fire pelted past me. I jumped into the blackness, and out of the corner of my eye I saw two soldiers on the deck of the last tank. It turned back toward Nafah, then disappeared. It was clear to me that we had been badly hit, and that I had to gather up the rest of the soldiers and return to the Nafah area. The groans of the wounded merged with the shrieks of the shells. I walked among the damaged tanks. My soldiers lay at the side of the ditch, some wounded, some no longer breathing. I made out Michael Naor, one of my platoon commanders. After bandaging his bleeding forehead, I concluded: "Apparently the Syrian commando unit from the Hermon ambushed us. Round up the wounded soldiers and go toward Nafah to call for reinforcements. I'll stay here to gather the rest of the company. When you return with the reinforcements, be sure not to shoot at us by mistake. We'll be walking along the fence." I thought naively that our entire brigade was already at Nafah, and that they would send us additional forces.

To be on the safe side, I checked my personal weapon, an Uzi submachine gun slung over my shoulder, but unluckily I discovered that its barrel was not functioning. Then I remembered a film about the Second World War that I had seen on Rosh Hashanah with Bella. In the film, the tanker took a 0.3 machine gun with a cartridge belt off one of the tank turrets and put it around his neck. I decided to follow his example. I ran to my tank, or more correctly, to what was left of it – a giant with a sloping barrel going up in flames that danced against the background of the night. From within it I could hear explosions and the shattering of bullets blowing up in the inferno. In my mind arose a pleasant memory of the popcorn we would make at home in the evenings while sitting in front of the TV and watching movies. But the acrid smoke scorched my lungs and brought me back to reality.

I climbed onto the tank to remove the commander's machine gun. The moment I stood on the deck, I heard a powerful explosion, and an enormous mushroom of fire burst from the turret. A wave of heat engulfed me, my vision blurred, and I could not tell whether this was reality or whether I was inside one of the horror films I so enjoyed. When I opened my eyes, I found myself lying at the base of the burning tank. My body was pinned to the ground, and my ears filled with a horrible rustle that bored into my brain, hissing mercilessly. "Stop!!" I screamed, hitting my ear and trying to stab at it with the small stalk of a plant, to no avail. The rustling noise drove me mad as shells continued to explode inside the tank. Finally I realized this was not a film, and that I had to act fast, for soon the tank would explode and fourteen tons of steel turret would fly into the air and land square on top of me. "You have no chance against it. Move away from here, get away," I muttered to myself, crawling with the remains of my strength toward a stony pile of dirt.

An enormous boom woke me from my blackout. I opened my

eyes and looked at my watch, which had stopped at 3:30 A.M. Dawn rose in a gray light, the air was thick with soot, and the burning seared smoke and flames burned my nose and lungs. I raised my aching head with difficulty, and my eyes beheld Syrian tanks and infantry. "No doubt I've made a navigation mistake and crossed over into Syrian territory," I thought. I scanned my surroundings, trying to reconstruct my path and search for familiar points. To my surprise, everywhere I looked I saw recognizable locations: to the north the houses of Nafah, on the east the mosque of Hushniye, and behind me Mashta. If I was determining my position correctly, I had not erred in my navigation.

I tried to organize my thoughts. How could it be that all the Syrians were on our side? By this time I was totally confused. Where were all the powerful tanks of the Israel Defense Forces? Where was the air force? And what in the world was I doing there, between the Syrian forces shooting northward and our forces returning fire from the direction of Nafah?

I continued to lie flat, helpless. Artillery fell around me from the sky, the ground shook and clods of earth flew on top of me. Airplanes exploded in the air and pilots parachuted down from them. Within all this tumult, I found myself lying at the edge of a rock with a weed in my ear, trying to stop the horrible rustling noise that was driving me out of my mind. Suddenly, I saw columns of Syrian tanks moving undisturbed toward the west, in the direction of the Kinneret. I hid among the rocks. There in the ground I buried all the written material I had received from the brigade, as well as my personal identification, so that they would not, Heaven forbid, fall into the hands of the enemy.

TAKEN PRISONER

Among my burned-out tanks, still spewing flames and black smoke, a column of Syrian tanks advanced on the Tapline Road toward Nafah. Suddenly I thought I heard the noise of a tank starter. I pressed hard on the rustling ear so I could focus on what was going on around me. I heard the sound of trampling on stones right beside me. I raised my eyes, and above me stood a Syrian soldier wearing an army sweater. He had a blackened face, a corporal's insignia on his arm, and a pistol in a holster on his belt. He looked at me with eyes wide in terror, moustache trembling. He raised his hands in surrender. I could not believe my eyes. There I was lying burned and wounded, weaponless and with a weed in my ear, not knowing a word of Arabic, and this Syrian soldier was standing over me like a statue, completely exposed to the shells falling all around. I signaled for him to lie down beside me so that the Syrians would not aim at us.

Then he realized I was wounded and weaponless. He lowered his arms, pulled out his pistol, and pushed a cartridge inside. Then he cocked the pistol and aimed it at me, shaking with tension. "Are you crazy! Move that pistol, don't you know you're not allowed to aim a weapon?! You'll let loose a bullet and cause a disaster!" I yelled at him in Hebrew, as if he were one of my soldiers. For his part, he gave back just what he had got, and began to shout in Arabic. Out of the mishmash of sentences he spat out, I caught the words "Anwar" and "Kalashnikov." Before he had finished, I found myself surrounded by Syrian soldiers aiming their Kalashnikov rifles at me. They searched me, kicking away the keys to the new apartment I had purchased shortly before leaving and had not yet had time to enjoy. Then they hoisted me off the ground, dragged

15

me to the nearest tank, and followed the tank commander's orders to throw me onto the turret like a sack of potatoes.

A young officer jumped from the tank, looked at me, and without a word went back inside and came out again with an aluminum container. He opened the cap, which also served as a mug, filled it with water and asked me in English if I wanted a drink. "Yes, please," I answered politely and gulped it down in one swallow. He poured me another cupful, and I swallowed that one down greedily as well. As I drank, the thought flashed in my head that I could not fight them, but I could finish all their water. So when I was done drinking the second cupful, I asked for a third. That one I barely managed to finish. In the meantime, the officer spoke on the radio, and finally told me in English, "Everything is okay, you can go." At least that is what I understood.

"I'm going toward Nafah, so tell your soldiers not to shoot at me," I said innocently in my broken English.

"Don't worry," he laughed, "the crew of the tank that brought you here will take you." He gave orders in Arabic to the crew members and pointed to the east. Then we began to walk. I was in shock at the number of Syrian forces present in the area. "Anwar" turned out to be the name of the tank driver, who knew about as much English as I did. I asked him what day it was. It seemed to me that many days had passed since we had left Tel Aviv. "Today is Sunday, and the time is 9:30 A.M.," he informed me. Shocked, I bumped into a rock and fell. So much had happened and only one day had passed? The Syrian crew lifted me up, and after walking for a while we arrived at a Syrian battalion aid station set up in the field. Stretchers with wounded men lay scattered on the ground. We heard cries and groans from all around.

All of a sudden, a tall Syrian rose from among the wounded. A Kalashnikov hung off his shoulder and a first lieutenant's insignia decorated his shoulders. He stood in front of me and began speaking to me in Arabic. I did not react, because I could not understand a word he was saying. Then he took the Kalashnikov down off his shoulder and hit my arm with the butt. Meanwhile, the Syrian crew stood behind me and watched what was going on, silent. I turned to Anwar and asked him to tell the man to stop hitting me because I was an officer, but another blow struck me, this time on the strap of my metal watch. The watch sprung to the ground, and the Syrian first lieutenant pounced on it as if it were precious booty and dropped it into his pocket. "Give me back my watch! That was a present from my parents for my bar mitzvah. I won't let you take my watch!" I screeched in Hebrew like a child whose beloved toy had been taken away.

The Syrian retreated two steps and loaded the Kalashnikov. Then he cocked it and began to spray bullets at my legs. I was frozen in fear and unable to react, but the Syrian crew members jumped toward me and protected me with their bodies. Then they took me away, yelling and waving their arms in the air at the lieutenant.

We walked for some time until we reached the area of Hushniye, where a Syrian tank was positioned at an observation post pointing west. On it stood about five soldiers with binoculars.

Suddenly, a giant burst from the tank. He had a huge head and a thick black moustache decorating his mouth. Behind him came a soldier who looked like a dwarf by comparison, despite his average size. The giant fixed his fearsome eyes on me and gave me a tremendous slap. I swayed like a leaf in the wind. My head spun, millions of tiny stars darted before my eyes, and I tumbled to the ground with a resounding thump. Wonder of wonders, the infuriating sound in my ears disappeared as if it had never existed. I smiled to myself in satisfaction. Then the giant lunged at me, grabbed what was left of the overalls on my body, and threw me in the air like a bag of feathers. He hurled me to the ground, lifted me up again, and finally stood me next to him. He cocked his pistol and rammed the barrel against my right temple. I closed my eyes. Pictures from my childhood and from the army flashed through my mind as in a film.

Israel's Independence Day, the IDF *parade in Tel Aviv.*
"Daddy, look how big they are," I say in excitement, pointing

toward the column of tanks approaching us. This is the first time I have ever seen a tank. When I'm a soldier, I'll command of one of those, I promise myself. Daddy says, "Let's hope that by the time you get to the army, we won't need tanks anymore…" But we do need them. I firmly refuse to join the navy. I want the Centurion, Battalion 82, Brigade 7th…My dear comrades…Tubi, I tried to save you. At least you got to eat. Everything is burning. My Centurion, where's my Centurion? I love you Bella, and you too, Raviv. Take care of Mom and your sister when she is born. Mom and Dad, be strong, I'm sure you'll manage without me…

As I awaited the sound of the shot, parting from my life and my dear ones, I felt a light tap on my arm and opened my eyes. The smaller man stood next to me and said in mangled Hebrew, "The commander says you should pray."

In my position, with a pistol pressed to my temple, I no longer cared about anything. "Tell him it's not fair," I said, and closed my eyes again, waiting for the shot. But for some reason the pistol barrel was removed from my head. Astonished, I looked up, and saw the giant smiling at me as he disarmed his pistol.

Then the smaller man, who was an interrogator or a translator, asked me in literary Hebrew, "Pray tell me, what rank do you bear on your shoulders?" My epaulets were torn and burned, obscuring the rank. "I'm a *seren* (captain)," I showed them, extending three fingers. "A *seren*." The man nodded his head and continued, "Pray tell me, what is the '*seren*' you bear on your shoulders?"

Then I recalled the term in English: "Captain, captain. Three stripes." The giant smiled at me. His eyes brightened, and he unbuttoned the buttons of his windbreaker and handed it to his companion. Then he began to take off his sweater. I did not understand why he was undressing in the middle of a war, and while the sweater covered his face, I dared to ask the translator, in Hebrew, "What's he doing? Why is he undressing? This is a war!" "Shhhh…" he hushed me, placing his finger on his mouth. I was sure I was in trouble and kept quiet. Then the giant finished his display, and stood wearing a beige Dacron shirt with three small stars on the epaulets. I assumed their insignia was equivalent to the Israeli system, and concluded he was a colonel. The monster slapped his chest in pride and shouted, *"Wa ana kaman kaptan* (I'm a captain, too)." I did not understand much Arabic, and because I heard him say *kaman* (the IDF acronym for "intelligence officer"), I concluded he was the regional intelligence officer.

The two Syrians fell silent, and I was sure that now they would begin interrogating me. Sure enough, the translator turned to me and said, "Pray tell me, what is your documents?" I told him I didn't understand the question. He got angry and repeated firmly, *"Dir balak* (damn it), answer me! What is your documents?" To this day I have no idea what he meant, but I answered him that I had no documents.

For a few minutes we held a pantomimed conversation and tried to understand each other. Then they tied my hands behind my back with telephone wire. The giant signaled to someone from the tank to get down. He gave him orders and sent me off, hands bound, with the new escort, a slim young man with no rank whose English was excellent. Apparently he was a propaganda officer. On the way, I told him about the Syrian soldier who had shot at me, and he told me not to worry. When we got to the battalion aid station, he sat me down on the ground. Suddenly I noticed the soldier who had shot at me, and I hinted this to my escort. The slim soldier went up to him and they exchanged a few words. Then they both came to me. "The soldier who shot at you begs your forgiveness," said the slim one, and I replied that I forgave him. As we were talking, the aggressive soldier took my watch out of his pocket and offered it to me, but before I could take it, my new escort preempted me and stuck it into his own pocket. This incident restored some of my self-confidence and offered me the hope that they were somewhat human. A few hours later, a Syrian armored personnel carrier (APC) arrived. They blindfolded me with a rag they picked up off the ground, and we rushed toward Syria, trying to dodge IDF fire.

After crossing the border, they took me out of the APC, and a group of Syrians gathered around me. From time to time they hit me on the head and shoved me in the shoulder with an iron rod. Someone pulled at my dog tag and asked, "*Inglezi*? American?" The whole time they also asked me, "*Tayr* or *malah*?" I did not understand. What did they think, that I was a tourist (*tayar* in Hebrew)? On reflection, I concluded that *tayr* must be "pilot," as in *tayara*, the Hebrew slang word for "kite" which was derived from Arabic. If so, then certainly all the Syrian forces I had seen going west had arrived in Haifa and Nahariya by now. They must have taken navy sailors, and this apparently was what they meant by *malah* (Hebrew for "sailor"). Later I learned that *tayr* was indeed "pilot," but *malah* meant "navigator."

We switched vehicles several times during the day. In the evening we arrived at a military camp in Damascus, where they untied my hands and took the blindfold off my eyes. We walked along a fence covered with a delicately scented sweet pea vine, and I enjoyed the feeling of being unbound. We entered a narrow room lit with bright neon lights. Along the wall was a long chest of drawers, and on it were tiny demitasse coffee cups and paper plates with crusts of bread. At the end of the room stood a table covered with a white tablecloth. They sat me in the single chair that stood on one side of the table. The other side of the table had two chairs. In each corner of the room stood a military policeman wearing a red beret and holding a Kalashnikov.

After a short wait, during which I peeled some strips of scorched skin from my hands, two men entered the room. They wore civilian suits – dark jackets with white shirts and ties – and carried leather briefcases. One looked to be about forty years old and had Arab features, while the other was young, tall and handsome. He looked like a Yemenite Israeli, and he had a warm, charming smile.

The "Yemenite" spoke Hebrew almost like a native. He asked for my name and whether they had treated my wounds. After I said I had received no treatment, he opened the door and spoke

with someone in the hallway. A few seconds later, they brought in
a plastic dish full of water. The Yemenite dipped a rag filthy with
blood into the gray water and began to wipe my face and neck.
My wounds ached and stung badly. I told him not to worry, that
I felt fine, and pushed his hand away from me. He flashed me his
charming smile and sat down across from me. This whole time the
older Arab had been staring at me with a cold, penetrating look.
He sat down next to his colleague. Then the "Yemenite" asked me
apologetically if anyone had offered me a drink.

"What can you offer me?" I asked.

"We have tea or coffee," answered the Yemenite.

"Does the coffee come in those little demitasse cups on the
chest of drawers over there?" I asked in a joking tone. Again in
a tone of apology, he answered me that that was how they drank
coffee.

"If so, then I would prefer tea," I replied, and in a few minutes,
they served me a small cup with tea so sweet I almost choked.

"That's how we serve *chi*," the Yemenite explained. Then the
older Arab interrupted by pounding on the table. He roared at me,
"*Bas!*" and spoke a few more sentences in Arabic.

The translator's face became serious. He bent down to his brief-
case and removed a cardboard file, opened it and told me he had
to fill in some information.

"What is your name?"

"Amnon Sharon," I answered, "army ID number 964508, rank –
captain, live in Tel Aviv."

"To which brigade do you belong?"

I explained that I was a tank commander in the reserves and
that he should not ask me anything else because I would not dis-
cuss the army. He translated what I said to his colleague. Then he
replied that the army did not interest them, that they only needed
a few technical details for the personal file.

As an armor officer, I had never received any training or preparation for being taken captive. I only remembered from newspapers
and films that if a person is captured, he should request a meeting

with the Red Cross. I did not know what this organization was and how exactly it could help me, but I told the Yemenite that if he continued talking about the army, I would demand they bring me the Red Cross. He relayed my request, and when he completed the sentence with the words *salib al ahmar*, which means "the Red Cross," they both burst out laughing. I got carried away and said, "Tell me *dogri* (seriously), when one of your officers is taken prisoner by us, does he give away information about the army?" Suddenly they fell silent and exchanged glances. The older Arab whispered something in the Yemenite's ear, and the latter began to speak in fluent Arabic. I was certain that he was continuing his conversation with his comrade, but then he switched to Hebrew and said, "I'm talking to you. Why aren't you answering me?"

"Listen, you made a mistake and spoke to me in Arabic," I answered, not comprehending what he was getting at. In the blink of an eye, the sweet smile disappeared from his face and his face was terrifying, his eyes hurling evil. "You're a liar, a liar! I know you're really an intelligence officer and you know Arabic. You said *'dogri.'* Speak Arabic now!" he insisted, pointing an accusing finger at me. I was shocked. How did they arrive at such a conclusion from one simple word? "*Dogri* is a word in Hebrew," I tried to explain. "I don't know Arabic, I'm just an armor officer in the reserves and I don't even know what an intelligence officer is!" The atmosphere in the room grew heated. They rose from their seats and shouted at me, insisting that I knew Arabic and was on the intelligence staff. I stuck to my side of the story. The pressure was unbearable. Their eyes flashed with fury. My body began to shake and I felt the ground dropping out from under my feet. In the end, I broke. I just didn't care anymore. "Okay, I'll tell you everything I know in Arabic," I said, capitulating. The two of them fell silent, and the young interrogator bent toward the senior one and whispered something to him.

"So, talk! Talk!" they urged me impatiently.

"But you should know that I don't even know what this means, and if it's something rude, then understand that I don't mean it against you."

"Go ahead, talk already," the interrogator encouraged me.

"All I know is *kus umak* and *kus uhtak* [curse words], and I don't even know what they mean."

Then what I had feared would happen came true. The senior investigator got up and bellowed something, and two soldiers ran toward me. They put a black sack over my head, grabbed my arms, hauled me up from the chair and dragged me with the soles of my feet barely touching the floor. I did not hear the door open, but from the strong scent of sweet pea and the cold wind blowing, I understood that I was outside the room, on my way to the unknown.

From a distance, terrifying shrieks erupted, approaching gradually until I could hear them right beside me. They took me inside that horrific place, undressed me and pushed me roughly onto the floor. I wore nothing but my underwear and the black sack over my head. I lay hunched in the total darkness, terrified, not knowing where I was or who was close by. The contact with the cold floor intensified the pain of my wounds and the friction on my scorched skin. To this the jailers added kicks, punches over my entire body, beatings with iron rods, and whippings with rubber hoses and sticks. Apparently I fainted from pain, because someone poured water on me to wake me up. A hefty Syrian soldier jumped on my chest, and I heard my ribs cracking. Sharp pain sliced through my body. "Speak Arabic!! Speak Arabic!!" someone screeched in my ears, and with my last strength I cried out, God, help me speak Arabic, just make them leave me alone…

They did not leave me alone, but rather lay me on a revolving machine, bound my hands and feet and turned me around at dizzying speed. My muscles stretched and my wounds tore. The upper half of my body felt like it was coming apart from the bottom half. With each rotation, they whipped the soles of my feet, and sharp currents of pain shot through my limbs like electric shocks. My senses began to blur. A screen of blackness enveloped me, and the voices around me grew farther away until they disappeared entirely. Cold water and kicks woke me up from my pleasant blackout, then more shouts, curses, and whippings. Blood streamed from my body. Again I screamed with all my might, calling out to God to help me, and then I fainted.

I awoke on the floor in a small room. A Syrian soldier bent over me and dressed me in a beige Syrian uniform. He removed the black sack from my head, and I could see my blood streaming from my open wounds and bruises staining my entire body.

When he was finished, the soldier sat me on a chair, but I fell forward like a rag doll. He picked me up, sat me in the chair again and supported me from behind, but my head still drooped forward. Then the door opened and a man in civilian clothes entered. He had a camera around his neck and lenses in a case hung over his shoulder. "Lift your head, I want to take your picture," he instructed me in English.

"I don't care about your picture!" I replied. "My face is dripping with blood and you're talking to me about a picture?!"

"It's worth it. This is your insurance policy," he tried to convince me, and although I did not understand exactly what he meant, with a monumental effort I lifted my head, and he photographed me.

The moment the photographer left, the tortures continued. They put the black sack back on my head and removed the Syrian uniform. I remained in only my underwear, and I could see nothing going on around me. Again the whippings, beatings, kicks and curses. I screamed in horror. The pain and the humiliation were too much to bear. I felt deceived: just a minute ago they had returned my humanity to me, and already they were taking it away again! When they had finished venting their wrath, I put on what was left of my shredded overalls and they took me to a car that drove me to the prison.

IN SOLITARY CONFINEMENT

We arrived at the prison. Outside it was bitter cold, and inside the moldy concrete walls, the cold penetrated even more deeply into the bones. The military police pounced on me like wild animals attacking their prey. They ripped off the remains of my overalls, then tossed me into solitary confinement like a pack of dogs stashing the remainders of their feast for later. Once again I was left naked except for my underwear, warmed only by the intense pain and the burning of my wounds.

The narrow solitary cell had a concrete bench and a steel door with three triangular holes. Every once in a while it would open, and a prison guard would enter carrying a stick or a rubber hose like an irrigation pipe. He would beat me on the face, head, back, and legs, then leave without a word, as if he had just finished a visit to the neighborhood fitness club. From the adjoining cells along the corridor I could hear shrieks and moans of pain. I did not know who my neighbors were. But the next day, apparently during the changing of the guard, fragments of sentences echoed from the cells. "Guys, anyone here from 117th?" "I'm from 102th." "And I'm from 119th."

I went to the door, placed my mouth on the openings of the little triangular holes and shouted, "I'm from 179th!" "Never mind him, he's from the greens," I heard one of them say, and I understood that they were pilots. To me, pilots have always been special people, and I was not the only one who thought that way. They were the elite of the IDF, and they enjoyed special treatment everywhere they went. I was not jealous of them, nor was I angry at the condescending tone from the neighboring cell. Rather, I decided to learn from them. I knew that they had undergone training for being taken captive, while I knew nothing about it. I thought they must be speaking in code, and made up my mind to listen to them in order to learn and decode it.

Later the guards returned. The heavy doors opened one after the other, and from the cells I could hear beatings and screams that gradually came closer to me. I trembled with fear; I had no idea what was going on just a few meters away from me. Then the door of my cell opened as well. I clung to the wall, my teeth chattered and cold sweat covered my naked body. I closed my eyes tightly, and suddenly I felt the blows of a thick stick on my face and body. I shrieked in pain and stretched out my hands in front of me in order to protect myself. Then I apparently grabbed the stick, and the Syrian soldier interpreted this as a counterattack. He ran from the cell with strident cries, and within seconds ran back with more soldiers. I threw the stick on the ground and three of them jumped on me and kicked me, beating me with rubber hoses and whipping me with a metal cable that cut into my flesh. I twisted and screamed, until one of them stuck his army boot into my mouth. My lips tore, and I choked. Slowly the voices moved away, the door closed, and I lay unconscious and bleeding on the cold floor of the cell.

The next day, they brought me a jug of water and tossed me a dry pita that I was unable to eat. They put a black sack over my head and took me out to the filthy, primitive latrine, where they gave me back my torn overalls and ordered me to get dressed. Then they bound my hands behind my back and led me to a car. After a short drive, the car stopped with a screech and they threw me into another solitary cell. The story repeated itself – they stripped, beat and cursed me. They threw me, still bound, onto the concrete floor. With each tiny movement I made, pieces of gravel and glass fragments protruding from the floor cut into my flesh.

Here, as in the previous cell, soldiers came in every half hour and beat me as I contorted on the floor. Blood flowed everywhere. I screamed in pain, and here as well, I could hear the same shouts and beatings from the other cells, with no relief in sight.

In the evening, they again covered my face with a black sack and dragged me to the interrogation room. From what I could hear and make out, I understood that I was near a table with about five men sitting around it. They stood me in the middle of the room, barefoot and wearing only my underwear. Behind me and on both sides of me stood guards holding whips, daggers, knives and other tools of devastation that they used on me when the muse inspired them. From the ceiling dangled a thick rope with an automobile tire tied to the end, like the swings that monkeys play on in zoos to make the audience laugh. As a youth I used to love American action and horror films, and here I found myself starring in one of them, complete with interrogators, torture instruments and hangman.

"What's your name, your rank and to which unit do you belong?" one of them asked me in Hebrew. Since when did they speak Hebrew in American films? I paused for a moment, uncomprehending, but a painful strike on my shoulder pushed me back to reality. "I'm Captain Amnon Sharon, an armor officer in the reserves," I said shortly. Activity began around me, but I could see nothing.

Suddenly someone threw me in the air, jammed me into the tire dangling from the ceiling, and whirled it around while the soldiers stood on all sides and beat me with iron rods. My head spun dizzily and I could see nothing. I could only feel the blood flowing from my wounds.

> *No, I'm not afraid to die. I've always been strong. I'm the son of a family that survived Auschwitz, that conquered evil and resurrected itself gloriously. They will not beat me. If only it didn't hurt! Where will the next blow come from? When will they let me out of here? What do they want from me? God help me!*

Several days, a seeming eternity, had passed since I had tasted food fit for a human being – the challah bread sandwich made by the mother of my tank driver, Karasenti. If I had known then that it was to be my last bread before my descent into hell, I would have eaten it bit by bit and enjoyed every crumb. The smell of the Iraqi pita they had tossed into my cell like a bone to a dog awoke in my memory the homey taste of that sandwich.

What is my wife Bella doing now? How is her pregnancy coming along? And little Raviv – who is taking him to nursery school? Mom and Dad, I know you're worried, but I'm sure everything will be all right. Remember? We always said that. Don't worry, I'm strong, I've never been sick, and you were always proud of that fact. Why do they beat me all the time? Why do they keep waking me up right after I faint? Just to go to the bathroom? That's what they do to little kids so they won't wet the bed!

They took the ropes off my hands to go to the latrine, but as soon as I had relieved myself, they bound me again and took me back to the solitary cell. I crawled to the jug of water they had brought with the pita. Gripping the rim with my teeth, I turned it upside down, and somehow managed to drink. My lips were still cracked and bleeding from the army boot incident. I grasped the jug with my teeth, and my blood flowed inside and filled it. As I drank, cries of pain again rose from the adjacent cells. Again the door of my cell opened, they covered my head with the black sack and took me to interrogation. Then they removed the sack. The lighting in the room was weak, and the tires dangling from the ceiling dizzied me once again. The interrogators asked about the brigades I knew. They shined projector lamps into my eyes, and within the blinding light I could see only blackness. My stomach ached with hunger. I awaited the moment when I could finally taste the pita they had thrown into my cell.

Finally they took me back to the cell with my hands bound behind my back. Again I clenched my teeth on the rim of the jug, and gulped the remainder of the water and blood inside. Then I crawled toward the pita. I tried to bite it, but it was as dry and hard as plywood. The following day, when they brought a fresh pita, I devoured it like an animal.

Almost a week has passed since I said good-bye to Amnon. He got his things together, caressed my stomach, and said, "Everything will be all right." I had the feeling that this time it wasn't just an operation but worse – a war. When the sirens blared I ran to the shelter with Raviv. He was not too scared, because he knew that Daddy was protecting us. I was also fairly calm. Amnon's Centurion was a seasoned combat warrior that none could overcome. He had escaped direct hits in the Six-Day War. How could the Syrians defeat him? At work my fellow teachers told me that their husbands had sent letters and called. Some had even come home on leave. Only I had nothing to tell. The days passed, and Raviv began to ask, "Mommy, why are all the daddies coming home and only my daddy doesn't come?" "He'll come, he'll come," I would encourage him, but inside me the fear began to take root.

I began to suspect that the worst had happened, but shared my fears with no one. I decided to keep going as usual, no matter what. Or perhaps I just did not grasp what was going on, for we were so young, in our twenties. I asked the many friends from the army who came to visit to stop coming. I did not want them feeling sorry for me. I only wanted to be by myself, or with my son and my parents. But at night, when lying in our double bed, as I hugged Amnon's pillow and felt the movements of the baby in my stomach, a film of tears would cover my eyes. What's the point of this pregnancy? I asked. Raviv has no father, and when this one is born, neither will it.

Darkness. The sharp shards of glass ruptured my wounds as I contorted on the cell floor. I touched my broken body to ensure that everything was in place. I recalled how two days before the war,

on Thursday afternoon, I had walked down Allenby Street in Tel
Aviv on my way to a meeting for work. I had stopped in front of the
display window of the Kapulsky pastry shop. Inside the window, I
could see middle-aged salesladies weighing the pastries behind the
counter. A glass goblet in the window held a colorful dessert that
drew the attention of the passersby. I stood in front of the dessert,
thrilled, and felt my craving for it intensify. "How much does this
cost?" I asked the saleswoman. "Ten *lirot*," she answered with an
embarrassed smile, as if sharing in my regret. Indeed, this was an
enormous sum, as that day I had eaten an entire steak lunch for
only one and a half *lirot*.

I continued to nurse my bleeding wounds and regretted not
having eaten that dessert... Morning came and a new day began.
This day was a bit different from the previous ones – I merited a
new method of torture. They lay me down on the ground, lifted
my feet and beat the soles with sticks, rods and rubber hoses. They
called these beatings "*falakot*," and they were particularly difficult
to bear, since the soles of the feet contain clusters of nerves that
affect the entire body.

In the breaks between interrogations, two Syrian soldiers came
in every few minutes and beat me from head to toe with rubber
hoses. They passed from cell to cell. All of a sudden, I heard shouts
from the neighboring cell: "Guard! Guard! I want to go home! I
live in Rishon Le-Tzion, it's near Rehovot!" Because of his shouts,
the guards would come and do another round. I concluded the
young man must be a pilot, and I was sure this was a trick he was
playing on them, part of some survival plan. Whatever might happen, I began to practice this trick, and repeated to myself, "I live
in Nahalat Yitzhak, it's near Tel Aviv."

After a while, I began to notice that the interrogations were
of a regular length. Sometimes the interrogators even stopped in
the middle of a sentence because the time was up. When they took
me back to the cell, I began to practice challenging words in literary Hebrew that I had learned from crossword puzzles, in order
to confuse the enemy. In one interrogation, for example, I used

the word "entreat," and thus enjoyed an hour of respite while they were busy searching for the definition of the word. In another interrogation, they asked me about the composition of the steel used in the tank. I had no clue about the combination of metals, but I gave them an example: "It's like what's on a tortoise," I said. They thought "tortoise" was a code word, and they spent the rest of the interrogation trying to decipher it.

On Wednesday they gave me a "pedicure." The interrogator took a metal bar and inserted it under my toenails until they popped off. My feet were swollen and covered with blood. The pain was horrifying, and I screamed like a madman until I fainted. When I woke up, I found myself in the cell. The brisk movement between cells, the cries of pain and desperation of the prisoners, and the terror-inspiring steps of the soldiers made it hard for me to fall asleep. I lay with my eyes open and tried to recall what had happened to me in the last few days.

If I'm not mistaken, it's been a week since I left Tel Aviv. By the end of the first day I lost most of my soldiers, and I don't know what happened to the others. I've been in two prisons and proved to myself that I can withstand suffering as well as the pilots, even though I didn't go through training for being taken captive. Do they know what's happening to me at home? Why doesn't the Red Cross come to visit? Can it be that the Israeli government is neglecting us? I don't even know if the war is over yet. Sometimes they tell me that my family is dead. I don't believe them, but what if...? What's hardest to bear is the uncertainty and lack of control, but I promised Bella that I'd be okay and I'll do all I can to fulfill my promise. I won't leave her a twenty-four-year-old widow with two kids!

"Get up!" a fat, unshaven Syrian soldier cut off my thoughts. His open, rolled-up shirt revealed a hairy chest and arms. He held a black object in his hand, and I understood that my program of

tortures for that day had not yet ended. He helped me get up because my hands were tied behind my back. We walked together
along the corridor until we reached a room with a straw mat on
the floor and a small oil lamp for light. He smiled and began to
wave the black object over me. It was a long hose, electrified on
both ends. He flipped a switch on the hose and began to touch
me around the ears, on my back and groin, and on the soles of
my feet. A pleasant tickle passed through my body. It wasn't possible that he came to make me feel good, I thought – the machine
is probably broken. I distorted my face, acting like he was hurting
me and shouting, "Stop, enough! That hurts, I can't stand it! Stop,
God help me!" He kept laughing loudly, and after a few minutes
he returned me to the cell, closed the door and opened the door
of the neighboring cell. Shortly afterward I heard the anonymous
neighbor shouting and screaming as I had. That was the first time
I enjoyed myself in prison.

The next day, the interrogations continued, this time with my
eyes uncovered. In front of me stood a Syrian interrogator with
eagle eyes, a translator, and a quiet interrogator with Russian features – fair hair and blue eyes. "At the parachutists' conference the
week before the war, the chief of staff, Major General David Elazar,
announced that the parachutists were armed with a new weapon.
What is this new weapon?" said the translator, relaying the eagle-
eyed man's question, which struck me like thunder on a sunny day.
What did I know about the parachutists? I had not heard of any
new weapon. "I don't know," I answered, and that cost me vigorous
blows on the back and neck. "What do you want from me? I really
don't know!" I shouted. They grabbed my hands and the soles of
my feet and used cables to connect them to a machine. "They're
electrocuting me. In a minute I'll be charcoal," I thought, terrified.
"You want to know what the chief of staff said?" I screamed, and
the current stopped at once. "Yes, tell us about the parachutists'
new weapon."

"Ask the chief of staff, I can't be responsible for what he says…,"
I dared, in an attempt to postpone the end. But two or three sol-

diers jumped on me with kicks and beatings. They stuck a knife in my back, and…when I woke up, I was in the cell, and a medic was treating the deep cuts in my back with iodine and band-aids.

So the days and nights passed in the detention facility of the "Second Intelligence Organization." Although I received no news from Israel, I was sure that my loved ones, if they were still alive, were working to find out what had happened to me and bring me home.

More than two weeks have passed since the day Amnon went to war, and still we know nothing. Some of his friends have already returned home or called. Others are lying wounded in hospitals, and to our sorrow, some will not return at all. We refuse to think that Amnon might not return, for his very birth symbolized the victory of life. After the hell of Auschwitz, we made our way to Eretz Israel, penniless. When we arrived at the DP camp at Cyprus I was already in the advanced stages of pregnancy. Amnon was born there. We stayed in the camp for about four months, and on November 29, 1947, we immigrated to Israel. Amnon was only three months old.

He was always a strong, healthy child, but more than anything, he was responsible. He would always let us know where he was going and if he was going to be late. A young man like Amnon doesn't disappear for no reason, and if we haven't heard bad news, then he must be alive somewhere. Why doesn't our government do anything to find him? We decided to find out for ourselves what had happened to him, and went to the headquarters in the Golan Heights. We went to the officers and asked questions. They nodded their heads as if they shared in our distress, but didn't give us any information. Someone said that we should try Rambam Hospital in Haifa, maybe his wounded friends could help us.

At Rambam we met Uzi Mor, the battalion commander.

His hand was amputated and his eyes bandaged, but when we started talking to him, he recognized us and was pleased we had come. We had met Uzi before the war, because the battalion members were like brothers. "Don't worry," he said, "I saw Amnon in the turret after he took his driver out of the tank. I shouted at him to jump so he wouldn't get hurt…and then I was injured." He fell silent for a moment, and in an encouraging tone, he added, "He was probably taken prisoner." We asked for more details, and finally he told us that in the field they had found Amnon's shoes without laces. They assumed the Syrians had used the laces to tie his hands. Uzi's words encouraged us greatly. We believed that Amnon was alive, and awaited the official announcement.

AL-MAZEH PRISON, DAMASCUS

October 21, 1973. I "move house" again. They gave me back my ripped overalls with the unmistakable signs of battle. This time I didn't have to squeeze my way into them as at the beginning of the war. On the contrary, they were somewhat roomy. My captors covered my head with a black sack and forced me into the car, even though I wasn't resisting. We drove to Al-Mazeh, the military prison in Damascus.

The reception was especially violent. They took me up the steps to the solitary confinement cell. After they had released my hands from the chains and removed the black sack from my head, I asked the new guard for some water. He gave me a look of "how dare you," and kicked my neck with his heavy military boot. A trickle of blood sprayed on the wall; more dripped to the ground. "Please, a little water…," I pleaded in a hoarse voice. This was one of those times when a person starts to believe in angels or messengers from above. The first sergeant who passed by at that moment was just such an angel. He bent over me, lifted my head gently and asked in Arabic, "*Shu bidak*? (What do you want?)" "Water, water," I mumbled. He signaled something to the guard, who disappeared, and in a few seconds returned with a plastic container full of water. The first sergeant held it, allowing me to drink until my thirst was quenched.

The new solitary cell was as dark as the previous one. The one window facing the outside was covered with sealed plywood. No more than a weak light penetrated through the glass window above the door to the corridor. The cell was just slightly larger than a man: about six and a half feet (two meters) long and four feet

(1.2 meters) wide. The lower half of the high walls was painted a dark green, the upper half in white. Between those walls I felt like a mouse inside a narrow, high shaft. The big advantage of my new "home" was the cement floor. There were no glass shards to stick out of the floor and cut every part of my body, only gravel bumps. The afternoon and evening of moving day were very calm. I lay on the cold cement in nothing but my underwear, trying to find a position that would relieve my aching body. This was the first time I was able to lie down "at my leisure." I focused on the cracks in the high ceiling and tried to decipher the Arabic graffiti on the walls. Who knew if my predecessors in the cell had gotten out of here alive, I wondered, and swore to myself that they would not break me, no matter what.

Groans from the adjacent cells, the scraping of metal, and doors slamming open and shut cut off my reverie. The door of my cell opened, allowing cold air to penetrate inside. A Syrian soldier with an orange beret threw me dinner – a potato baked in its jacket. I hadn't eaten a vegetable for several days, so I enjoyed this delicacy. Before the door closed again, I could see the guards outside bundled in long coats, coughing, sneezing and spitting their phlegm on the floor. I was proud of myself that although I was wearing only underwear, I didn't even have a cold like they did.

Night. My neighbors in the nearby cells could not fall asleep. Once in a while jailers entered the cells, and I heard kicks and whippings, screams of pain, doors slamming, shouts in Arabic... The voices came closer and closer to me. I tried to hunch myself into the fetal position so I could warm up and fall asleep, but apparently the guards had other plans for me. Two of them entered my cell, and one spoke to me in Arabic while the other beat my face and head with a thick iron rod. I stretched out my hands to protect my face. Not missing the opportunity, he beat me on my palms as well. I almost ripped my lungs with my screams of pain. When finally they left me alone, they smiled in amusement, but not before granting me a parting kick. The pain was so intense that I felt my body and soul separate into two entities.

Bella also probably feels kicks in her stomach, from the baby. I see you, Bella, you're stroking your stomach and smiling with the pain. Raviv is lying next to you and puts his head on your stomach to hear his sister. I see that you're sad. Don't cry, Bella, I'll come back. It'll be all right. Remember the telepathy games we used to play? Close your eyes and concentrate. Yes, like that, do you see? I'm healthy and well. I don't even have a cold. Hold on, I promise I'll come back.

So passed the first night, and many more after it. Every half an hour the visits repeated themselves, along with the beatings and shouts. If I allowed myself to faint, someone was sure to wake me up right away and bring me back to reality.

Fifteen days have passed since we said good-bye. His parents continue to look for him tirelessly. I'm more limited – my stomach is swelling, and I have submerged myself in my work so as not to sink into black bitterness. His parents went up north and returned with a spark of hope that Amnon is in captivity, but we haven't received any official announcement yet. They mentioned a pair of shoes without laces that was found in the field, and concluded that they had tied his hands with the missing laces. I have nothing else to hold onto but that assumption. Sometimes in the evening, I lie on the bed and Raviv lies next to me and places his head on my stomach. Then I remember that Amnon also used to do that in the first pregnancy. He would always say to me, "It'll be okay, the baby will be born healthy and strong." Even now, in these difficult moments of uncertainty, I hear his voice, confident and soothing – "It'll be okay, Bella, everything's alright."

On the first day in Al-Mazeh prison, they woke me up with shouts and kicks in order to go to the latrine, and after that it was time for breakfast. On the floor in my cell, a Syrian soldier placed a deep dish of orange plastic. It contained steaming hot tea, and two thick pita breads, called *hubzim*, one on top of the other. Inside the top one was a handful of black olives. I pulled the dish full of tea to my mouth, and the scent rising from it was strong and sweet, like the tea they had given me in my first interrogation. I was pleased. This is the right thing at the right time, I thought; it will warm me up a little as well as clean out my insides. I swallowed carefully, and felt soft pieces inside my mouth. I looked into the dish, and my face fell: tiny worms were swimming inside it. I spat the ones I hadn't yet swallowed back in the dish, and in disgust I ate the pita breads with the olives, after checking that they didn't have live "nutritional supplements" as well.

When I was little, my mother used to have me breathe steam. "It's good for your health," she would say. "It opens your breathing passages. It's good for your lungs, and it cleans out the pores of your skin." I decided to try it. I closed my eyes so I wouldn't see the worms and breathed in the steam, and so I combined my meal with a steam treatment, getting two for the price of one.

That morning my luck improved, at least temporarily. They threw me a pilot's overalls, and as always they covered my head with a black sack and took me for interrogation. "Are you the pilot Dov Shafir?" the translator asked me. "No, I'm an armor officer in the reserves," I replied. I already anticipated the beating that would come after my denial, but suddenly someone lifted up the black sack from my head. I blinked in the sudden light and heard the translator confirm that indeed I was the officer from the armored corps reserve forces. They took me back to the cell. I returned the overalls to the jailer, and after the door locked, I lay back down on the cold floor and wondered what had happened to that pilot. I may even have caught some sleep.

When I returned to Israel, I was told that Dov Shafir returned along with us, but in a casket.

I woke up to the clatter of the dishes, and guessed it was time for lunch. Again they pushed an orange plastic dish into my cell. Inside it was rice with pieces of chicken skin and half an apple. I ate quickly, because as soon as they finished handing out the food to all the cells, they started collecting the plates.

At least things were boring until the afternoon, and I had free time to develop a system for keeping track of the days. According to my calculations, the date was October 22, a Monday, sixteen days since I had gone to war. I was sure that as the days passed, I would lose my sense of time. The dark cell made it hard to tell the difference between day and night. So I began to repeat to myself that now it was the afternoon of Monday, October 22. Every day I would repeat the day to myself this way, to the tune of the Simon and Garfunkel song, "Bye Bye, love." "Bye-bye, Monday; hello, Tuesday. I hope it'll be a good day, I hope it'll be a wonderful day..."

In the afternoon, they took me out for another interrogation. I stood as usual with a black sack over my head. Even before the interrogation started, two soldiers attacked me and beat me energetically over my entire body. After I collapsed, they continued to kick my head, back, legs and anywhere else they could. "Good God, help me!" I screamed helplessly, and someone poured a bucket of cold, stinking water over me.

"What brigades do you know?" asked the interrogator, and signaled with his head for one of the soldiers to beat me.

"Brigade 7," I answered, earning a slap.

"And which battalions?" he continued. From the tone of his voice I could sense a poisonous smile spreading on his lips.

"Battalion 82," I said honestly, and another punch landed on my head.

"Which others?" screamed the interrogator impatiently.

"I don't know the other battalions. What do you want from me?"

The beating continued, and I felt as if my body were dripping downward. It boiled from the blows, while the contact with the cold floor gave me chills. Someone lifted my legs and whipped the soles of my feet. God, how it hurt. Powerful currents coursed through my body like lightning, and sparks of fire flashed in my brain. My strength was gone. My body emptied, my breathing weakened... I woke up in the cell bruised, hurting, and dripping with blood. As I did after each interrogation, I felt my body with my hands to verify that all its parts were still in place. I thanked God with a prayer I composed at that moment, a variation on traditional formulas. I still recite it three times a day: "*Shema Yisrael* – Hear O Israel, the Lord is God, the Lord is One. Blessed are You, Lord our God, King of the universe, through whose word everything came to be. Blessed are You, Lord our God, King of the universe, through whose word everything is done. Lord God, give me strength to continue, keep me healthy, protect me and my family. Amen, amen, amen."

The last time I had prayed, I had been called up to the Torah, and I remembered the *Shema* from that synagogue experience. After praying, I felt better. I felt spiritual uplifting and relief, and willingly ate the cooked spinach leaves they gave me for dinner. After the meal I got organized for sleep, and even though I had been through a difficult day, I had a hard time falling asleep. I gazed at the ceiling and wondered what was happening in Israel and at home. Had the war ended? How had the holidays passed? I couldn't even wish my loved ones happy holidays.

I had never been an expert in religious matters, but because I had begun to repeat the dates, I remembered the approximate dates of the holidays. For some reason I remembered Sukkot a bit late, and this upset me deeply. Three weeks before the war broke out, we had moved into our new apartment in Nahalat Yitzhak, and I had promised Bella that during Sukkot we would have our *hannukat bayit*, our housewarming ceremony. I tried to recall what the apartment looked like, the building entrance, and how many solitary confinement cells my bedroom would hold. As I reflected, I hummed to myself the Russian song "*Lyushinka*" sung by popular vocalist Michal Tal: "Finally he came home / After so many years / He returned to you, Lyushinka / Why didn't you wait for him?" Hot, salty tears streamed down my face, stinging my wounds. Profound sadness and a powerful longing enveloped me. What if I really returned after many years, and no one was waiting for me?

On the eve of the holiday of Sukkot, I accompanied Raviv to nursery school as I did every day. In the yard stood a small sukkah decorated with the children's artwork. "Shalom, Raviv's grandfather, look what a beautiful sukkah Raviv made," said the teacher, pointing to one of the pictures. "He even drew Dad in a tank inside a sukkah." I felt a pinch in my heart, and asked if I could take the picture home. "But keep it for Dad," Raviv stipulated, and I promised I would. When Amnon was little, we used to go around the neighborhood to the different sukkot and give points, judging which one was the prettiest. This year people hadn't invested in their sukkot as much as in previous years, apparently because of the security situation. We all got together at our house for the holiday meal, and offered a prayer that if Amnon was in prison, it would be a temporary dwelling, like the sukkah. To us, the holiday expressed the concept of temporariness and longing for stability and peace.

Slowly the tortures became routine, and my daily schedule was regular. Three times a day the guard would throw me the black sack to put over my head, then lead me down the corridor to the latrine. There was no toilet or toilet paper, just a hole in the cement floor and beside it a short rubber hose attached to a faucet, like an improvised bidet. Outside it stood a stone sink with a small faucet for washing hands. The latrine ceremony lasted for a few minutes, after which they covered my eyes again and dragged me back to the solitary cell like a blind beast.

Meals were also served three times a day. The doors opened one after another, and we heard the rattling of plates and shouts in Arabic, after which they again latched the bolts. Shortly thereafter, the doors opened again and they gathered up the plates, even if we hadn't yet finished our meal. Every day we would get a piece of fruit for lunch, and every two or three days we received a piece of citrus fruit as well. As part of the "alternative medicine" I developed there, which included breathing steam from the wormy hot tea, I would squeeze the peels of the citrus and use the essence to sterilize my wounds. I also got used to the worms in the tea and spat them out skillfully, like I would do as a child with the onion my mother insisted on adding to the soup, "just for taste."

Later interrogation time would arrive. The suffering and the beatings I underwent in the cell were like nothing compared to those in the interrogations. Each time the door opened, my body shook in fear, for I did not know in what condition I would return to my cell. But I knew that even if I was pulverized and my ribs were broken, I would overcome. For each interrogation, I defined a threshold of pain for myself, and it increased from one interrogation to the next. Slaps, cigarette burns, *falak* beatings, electric shocks, spinnings – for all these I made a mental bet against the interrogators whether I would stand up to it or not, and I was pleased to discover that I was winning.

At night it was hard to fall asleep. Dogs barked outside. The guard who stood next to my cell on a regular basis loved music, and all night long he would sing nerve-racking songs in Arabic. Sometimes the guards would come into the cell. They would beat, spit, kick, and then leave. Exhausted and in pain, I made sure to repeat the date and say my prayer three times a day, hoping that tomorrow would be no worse. Finally I would fall asleep.

On October 28, just after breakfast, the guard came in and ordered me to stand with my face to the wall. He went out and locked the door behind him. I stood and stood and stood. My feet hurt, and I felt them gradually swelling. I tried to move and massage them, but I noticed that every few minutes the guard was looking in through the slit in the door. I couldn't hold myself up any longer, and after a few hours of standing I crumpled and lay on the floor.

No more than a minute passed when the door opened. Shouts, beatings, whippings, and I was on my feet again, gripping the damp wall with my fingernails so that I would not fall. I ate lunch standing up, and dinner as well. From time to time I grew sleepy and leaned against the wall, but the guard made sure to wake me up with beatings. After about fifty hours of standing, I fainted and fell face down on the rough floor. When the guard heard my fall, he entered the cell and began to beat me. He turned me over onto my back, and saw that blood was dripping from around my eyes and spreading all over my face. He called a medic, who cleaned my face and put iodine on every blood stain he could see. The second the medic left, the guard pulled me up onto my feet, and I continued to stand for seventy-two hours straight.

One day, they threw me a wool army blanket that stank of cigarettes and urine. I considered what to do with it. Should I use it as a mattress to protect myself from the pieces of gravel, or should I use it as a blanket to cover myself? Finally I decided to make it into a "blattress," or blanket-mattress, spreading one half on the floor and using the other half to cover myself.

The next week, they brought me another army blanket, and yet another during the third week. I wondered whether they were preparing us for the cold winter or whether they just wanted to get rid of a stock of blankets that were no longer serviceable. In the fourth week, a barber arrived. He shaved my head and face with a hand clipper, and when he was done with the haircut he slapped the nape of my neck with his palm and said, "*Na'iman*," a special blessing after a new haircut.

The daily interrogations continued, and sometimes even took place twice a day. When they were finished, I made sure to learn by heart all the lies I told the interrogators, so that I could stick to my story. I even began to get used to the *falak* beatings on the soles of my feet. If at the beginning I used to faint after three or four of these, with time I was able to hold out for more than ten.

In between interrogations I was very bored. I could not sleep, because despite the blankets they had given us, the late November cold was taking its toll. I lay on the cold floor, daydreaming.

In one of my dreams, I saw three corpulent Red Cross staff members with black moustaches. They told me that there was a war going on with Egypt and Syria, and that the government of Israel was negotiating with the government of

Egypt. The negotiations were proceeding sluggishly. Many discussions were held, some short, some long. The situation was sensitive and tense. "Are there prisoners in Egypt as well?" I asked them in my dream, and they confirmed that just now an exchange of prisoners was taking place between Egypt and Israel. "When do I return?" I wondered. "Syria and Israel have just begun negotiations regarding their exchange of prisoners, but in this case as well, the discussions are starting and stopping in the middle." It seemed as if they did not want to continue the discussion. Then the telephone rang. I was anxious to hear how the negotiations would conclude. The one talking on the phone smiled at me and said, "A date has been fixed for the exchange of prisoners between Syria and Israel: June 8." He did not mention which year, but I already saw myself at home.

The truth is that I had good reason to doubt the dreamed-of date. I remembered that in the past, I had read articles about prisoners of war and about their time in captivity. The prisoners of Operation Kadesh in 1956, for example, had returned to Israel after ten years, and the pilots taken in 1967 during the Six-Day War returned after four years. But logic showed that the length of stays in enemy prisons was declining over time, and that the date June 8, 1974, in another eight months, was definitely appropriate.

On November 17, according to my calculation, the door opened, and in the doorway I saw the interrogator who had been at my first interrogation together with the "Yemenite" translator. This time he was alone. He handed me new, light blue pajamas, still in their package, and closed the door. Between the folds I found a pin that I kept as a tool. I used it to scratch my name on the wall, to open wounds filled with pus, and to clean my fingernails. The pin was like a toy for me, and helped me to pass the time.

In November, we heard a rumor that in the basement of Tachbiv Hall on Ibn Gabirol Street in Tel Aviv there were photographs of the prisoners, taken by foreign reporters. I asked my wife to accompany me, but she said she would not be able to stand disappointment. So I went by myself. In the basement were tables with photographs of prisoners in Egypt and Syria. I was sure it would be a trivial thing to identify my son, for who knows a child better than his parents? I searched among them, but there were so many that I became completely confused. I could not tell the difference between any of the bearded, long-haired men in the photographs. I went home sad and disillusioned, but said nothing to anyone. Later my brother-in-law arrived. He had also gone to the basement, and brought me a picture of a bearded man. "I found this on the table of the 'Egyptians,'" he said, "I think it's Amnon." That evening we called Bella and told her there was a picture of Amnon. Despite the blackout at that hour, she came right away, and the moment she opened the door, she allowed us to turn on the lights. "It's Amnon!" she cried with complete assurance. In order to remove any shade of doubt, we went to Bella's parents.

Amnon's father Moshe arrived at our house after the blackout along with Bella. They brought a picture of a bearded man with long hair and a scared expression. Despite the poor quality, you couldn't mistake the light-colored eyes and stenciled eyebrows – it was Amnon. Moshe burst out in heart-breaking tears, and we after him. They were tears of fear mixed with joy, for until then we had received no proof that Amnon was truly in captivity.

December. The cold was unbearable. My skin prickled each time the guards' footsteps approached my cell. The tortures had become regular, but every once in a while they introduced a new horror. I sat hunched on the blanket that served as a mattress, waiting in fear for interrogation time. The door opened, and as usual they put the black sack over my head and took me to another interrogation. Once again, questions, beatings, kicks, whippings, *falak* beatings on the soles of my feet. Once again, I have nothing new to tell them; I really don't know anything!

"What kind of missiles do they have in the IDF?" asked the interrogator.

"I don't know," I replied. I was ready for the furious response, which was not late in coming. They beat me murderously, and I fainted. After they woke me up by slapping my cheeks, I decided to "break" and told them about the ss-11 missile, an anti-tank missile with a range of two kilometers (1.2 miles).

"What other missiles are you familiar with?" the interrogator insisted.

"I don't know," I whispered in a shaking voice.

"What's the ss-12?"

"That's an improved missile for three kilometers (1.9 miles)," I answered, pleased at my bright idea, but the interrogators were less pleased. The soles of my feet suffered ten *falak* beatings, perhaps even more, because I could no longer feel the rest. When I woke up in my cell, instead of the fruit as the extra dish at lunch, I found a sweet pastry made with honey balls, as if to sweeten the bitter interrogation.

In the middle of the month, they pushed a small towel with colored threads on the edges into my cell. That evening they put the black sack over my head, told me to take the towel and took me to the shower on the bottom floor. On the way I walked barefoot through puddles of muck, and pieces of something unidentified stuck to my feet. The shower cells were small and filthy. Wool blankets acted as dividers between the showers and prevented contact between the prisoners. I took off my underwear, placed it on the side next to the towel, and stood under the shower, which was operated from the outside by one of the jailers. A powerful jet of boiling water poured over me. I jumped aside before it could burn me. With my hand I splashed water onto my body. After a minute the shower stopped. A small, grainy piece of soap that reminded me of laundry soap flew toward me. I tried not to open the wounds that had scabbed, even though I had to scrub hard to get clean since I hadn't taken a shower for two months. I soaped under my armpit and felt my hand sink inside. I suddenly realized my condition – I, who had had a full and muscular body, was reduced to skin and bones. In two months I had lost all my extra body fat, and my muscle mass had gone limp. A torrent of boiling water washed away my thoughts, and I hurried to finish. They put the black sack over my head and walked me back to the cell through the same moldy puddles of water and mud.

After the shower, I felt that the chapter of the battle had been washed off me together with the dust, the soot, and the terrible images. I was ready for the next stage, the meeting with my family. I lay on the floor, wrapped myself in one of the blankets, closed my eyes and "talked" to Bella.

She told me that Raviv was still going to nursery school, and she, to her school. She said that the grandparents continued to help and that her stomach was swelling. She didn't say a thing about the efforts of the Israeli government to release the prisoners. I also told her about everything that had happened to me in the last few days, and about my dream last night: "You can go home for the weekend," said the jailer who stood all night long outside the door and sang annoying songs. He even handed me the key to a car, but warned me, "You must get back on time, because if not…" I didn't let him finish the sentence. I grabbed the key, and as I ran toward the car I shouted, "I promise!" I raced through the streets of Damascus, crossed the border without getting stopped and found myself in my neighborhood.

On the street near the house, crowds of people awaited me with flowers and "Welcome Home" signs. Children waved flags, just like on the Israeli independence day, Yom Ha-Atzma'ut. The new apartment was just as I remembered. The tables were full of flowers, people came in and out, and everyone cried with joy. I entered the room with Bella.

*Behind us were my parents, my sister, and Bella's father.
Raviv sat on his bed because it was late, and my mother-
in-law, who was taking care of him, hushed us. I went up
to Raviv on the tips of my toes and kissed him lovingly. The
meeting was deeply emotional, but I had to cut it off and
return to Damascus; otherwise another prisoner would not
be able to go on leave.*

I awoke with a start at the sound of the door bolts opening, and
stood in the corner of the cell. The night shift jailer had brought
a friend with him, and the two of them whipped the palms of my
hands with iron wires. I tried to hide my hands under the blanket
that covered me, but it fell off, and I was left exposed to their abuse.
One of them grabbed my hair, which was too long, and hurled my
head against the wall several times. A bloodstain appeared on the
wall, and large, red drops dripped onto the cement floor, form-
ing a small puddle. Finally they threw me to the floor, spat on me,
and left. I lay huddled and trembling with fear, trying to stop the
bleeding with my hand. I prayed that the wound would close and
scab, and that I would not lose too much blood.

Apparently the jailers were alarmed by the amount of blood
flowing from my head, for they decided to give me a break of two
days from the cell beatings and the interrogations. To pass the time,
I invented names for all of the regular jailers based on their job,
appearance, and behavior. There was "Abu Pajama," and "*Juhader*
(ugly)," a particularly hideous one. There was also "Kindhearted,"
who sometimes smiled at me and asked, "*Shu? Tamam*? (Is everything okay?)"

Once when there were no jailers around, I heard knocks from
the wall on the left. I knocked back with my fist and listened closely.
My neighbor answered me with return knocks, so I assumed he was
a pilot trying to make contact using prearranged signals, which I
unfortunately did not know.

The dream about the meeting with the Red Cross staff returned
again and again, especially on the days when they did not take me

to interrogations. I kept repeating June 8, which my dream had predicted as the date of my freedom. I encouraged myself that a quarter of the time, two months, had already passed, and the worst was certainly behind me.

As I was busy with my calculations and plans for the future, the door opened, and very quickly I was brought back to reality. Once again they put me into the tire hanging from the ceiling and interrogated me about the names of the brigades and battalions. In the midst of rotations as fast as a centrifuge, my head fell out of the tire. It wouldn't have taken much to rip it right off. They took me back to the cell. A jailer whom I had never seen before removed the black sack from my head and placed his two enormous palms on my ears. Then he spread his hands apart and brought them together in a mighty blow like a cymbal player. My temples pounded like hammers, my ears rang like church bells. The walls of the room began to spin, and the graffiti on the wall danced like demons. My sense of balance weakened, and I felt as if I were sinking down, down. With a mechanical gesture I stretched out my hand to the floor to stop my fall. In my confusion I said to myself, "Amnon, you can't fall, you're lying on the floor already." Then I fell asleep.

I was not able to eat lunch that day, but in the evening I forced myself to eat the serving of spinach. I prayed my evening prayer and fell into a deep sleep.

After breakfast the next day, I heard voices in the corridor, steps, and the unusual sound of the slits in the doors opening and closing. I stood tensed and ready for another round of bullying. The slit in the door of my cell opened, and a pair of eyes peeked in. "How are you?" someone asked me in clumsy English. I didn't want to tell him the whole truth lest they use it against me, so I said I felt a bit weak but aside from that everything was fine.

"I am a doctor and I shall give you some drugs," said the pair of eyes, closing the slit. He disappeared with his promise unfulfilled, and thus ended the first doctor's visit.

After this, the guards covered my head with the black sack and took me, as usual, to the interrogation room with my hands bound

behind my back. Someone pushed me forcefully to the floor, and
two soldiers kicked me all over my body. My mouth filled with
thick blood. The wounds that opened stung and bled as well. Suddenly one of the soldiers grasped my legs, and whipped the soles of
my feet. Sharp currents like electric shocks sliced through the entire length of my body up to my brain. I screamed in pain, writhed
and cried out to God to help me. They lifted me up and sat me on a
chair next to a table. I swayed like a pendulum. My rear hurt and it
was hard for me to sit down, but I decided not to break. I lifted my
head, straightened my back and waited. I heard murmurs around
me, and they lifted the black sack from my head. In front of me sat
a man with an Arab face wearing civilian clothes, and in one hand
he held a string of beads that he fingered.

"How are you?" he asked me in Hebrew. I nodded my head to
mean, "Okay."

"Do you have family? Parents? Brothers? Sisters?"

I answered that I was married with a son and that my wife
was pregnant.

"Are your parents alive?"

"Of course they're alive, may they live to 120," I answered right
away.

"Is your mother alive? Are you sure?" he asked, laughing sa-
tanically. Before I could ask him what he meant, they covered my
head with the black sack and took me back to the cell.

"They're probably trying to undermine my confidence, to
break me," I thought. "They won't get me down with this method."
I pushed away the bad thoughts, and tried to fall asleep by repeating the names of the Maccabi Tel Aviv basketball players.

In the afternoon, they took me for interrogation. Several
interrogators wearing uniforms were in the room. One of them,
"Eagle Eyes," as I had nicknamed him, asked me, "What is *Merkavah* (chariot)?"

"I don't know," I answered, and that was the truth.

"We know that you know. What is *Merkavah*?" he insisted,
maintaining a quiet but threatening tone.

"I once saw a brigade badge with a picture of a chariot, so maybe it's the name of a brigade," I replied innocently.

"Eagle Eyes" squinted in fury. He compressed his lips and signaled with his head to the two jailers who stood behind me. They bashed me with their clubs until I felt my bones breaking. As if that were not enough, they pushed my chair backwards, lifted the soles of my feet and… "Enough!!" I began to tremble, and screamed in desperation, "I don't know what it is!!"

"It's a type of weapon," the interrogator continued in his threatening calm, and nodded his head to the jailers as if dictating the pace of the beatings. While one of the jailers continued with the *falak* beatings, the other varied with kicks at my shoulder.

"A long time ago we had chariots with horses and spears, but we don't have those anymore," I tried to convince them with the last of my strength, even though I knew that was not the answer they wanted. The interrogator, who until now had seemed calm, lost control. He shoved back his chair in anger, came over to me and landed a powerful karate-chop blow on my neck. Inside the black sack, complete darkness prevailed. My head spun, and in the background the voices faded away. I began to appreciate those moments of disconnection, when nothing hurt anymore and my spirit wandered in other, more pleasant regions. But with admirable efficiency the jailers made sure that those moments did not last for long. Each time I fainted, they would pour a bucket of cold, stinking water on me. This time as well, I woke up sopping wet, and as they dragged me to my cell I heard the interrogator shout, "Don't you know there's a new Israeli tank, the Merkavah?"

Indeed, I did not know.

I lay in the cell, a shadow of my former self. My breathing was heavy, and stabbing pains pierced my chest. Maybe there really was a new Israeli tank? I fixed my eyes on the white ceiling, whose grooves recalled barren riverbeds.

Here I am in the Negev, standing on a hill in Area 302, which I know well from the many training drills. I wear the new stripes of a colonel on my shoulders. In front of me is a fleet of matchboxes, a cigarette sticking out of each one like the barrel of a cannon. These are my Merkavah "tanks." I point to them in pride and order, "We're going up north." At my command, the boxes begin to grow, and in the blink of an eye they are transformed into powerful tanks, like Cinderella's pumpkin turning into a beautiful carriage. I lead my private fleet through the city streets, and a great crowd cheers us in excitement. Dizengoff Street in Tel Aviv. The tanks tear up the road, Israeli flags wave in the wind, and the voice of the announcer echoes through the giant speakers. "You see before you the strongest tank in the world, the Merkavah!"

I stand on the turret, stretching on the tips of my toes, and find my father within the huge crowd. Beside him stands a boy about eight years old who looks remarkably like me. "Dad," I call out, and although he can't hear me, he raises his arms, claps his hands in enthusiasm and sends me a gigantic smile that says, "I knew it, son."

We travel the roads of Israel, going up to the Galil and conquering the Golan. When night falls, I say my prayer and snuggle up at the foot of my Merkavah.

By the end of January, I was a veteran after four months in solitary confinement. It was about time for an improvement in conditions. Indeed, one evening they threw a straw mattress into my cell. About eight centimeters (three inches) thick, it was stained and stank of urine and cigarettes. I spread one of my blankets on top of it and lay with my hands under my head, enjoying the upgrade. "Just like a five-star hotel," I thought. "Now I can stay here for a year!"

"Please, not a year," I reconsidered, terrified by the very idea. "But if I have to be here for such a long time, then at least they should allow me to correspond with home. That way maybe I'll be able to learn something about what's going on in the world." As it was, the only cultured person with whom I could communicate without getting beaten was myself. If I couldn't fill myself in on events outside my own realm, I could certainly encourage myself and work to preserve my sanity.

After a while, the mattress began to irritate me, and I had no choice but to spread all the blankets on top of it, except for one which I used to cover myself. As I had graduated from the textile program at ORT Shenkar vocational school, I thought I could find a solution to improve my sleeping situation, which soon became unbearable. At night, I imagined I was founding a factory for large, thick mattresses. The factory had gigantic looms that produced mattresses instead of rolls of cloth. Devoted workers stood beside each machine. Trucks delivered raw materials, then took away the completed merchandise for distribution throughout the country. This dream continued for many days, and in the end I was as exhausted as if I had really been working.

After a short break, they took me for interrogation again. As usual, the questions revolved around the brigades and platoons. Whenever my answers were unsatisfactory, they brought me a map and asked me to mark places in Israel where there were special installations like army bases, electricity plants, and gas storage tanks. Of course I did not mark strategic locations, but only places that were widely known, such as the Reading Power Plant in Tel Aviv, Julis army base near Ashkelon, and Nitzanim base.

"What do you know about Gelilot?" they asked me. "What kinds of installations and bases do they have there?"

"I remember that when I was a kid, there was a camp there called Jalil, where we used to have pre-military training through school," I said. As in previous interrogations, this earned me a violent reaction. Then they dragged me to the cell, battered and dripping with blood.

The next day, after lunch, they covered my head with a black sack and took me to the last solitary confinement cell at the end of the corridor. The door of the cell stood open, and inside waited a barber holding a hand clipper, ready for action. He shaved my face, and moved on to the right side of my head. The scabs that had not yet healed opened and began to bleed, and the barber mopped it up with a filthy rag. At a certain point the guard went up to the barber and whispered in his ear. The barber stopped his work and moved aside. The guard came to me, lifted my chin, looked me in the eyes and asked a question in Arabic. I didn't understand his question, so he repeated himself, and at the end of the sentence he said, "Israel, Syria? Eh?" I couldn't understand what he meant. I thought he was asking me who was better or stronger, Israel or Syria, so I answered, "Syria."

Silence. The barber approached me with a furious look, and stretched the hand clipper out in front of him like a sword. Then he and the guard jumped on me, threw me from the chair and beat me all over while cursing and swearing in Arabic. When they finished, the guard dragged me along the corridor back to my cell.

In the evening, the jailer brought in my dinner, a cooked sweet potato. He looked at me and burst out laughing. Then he went out of the cell and locked the door. "Maybe they put something in the sweet potato," I suspected, and began to peel it carefully to avoid any surprises. As I was peeling, I heard giggles from behind the door. I looked up and saw the slit open, and amused eyes peering inside. During the night, they kept peeking into my cell and laughing in ridicule. I couldn't fall asleep until I placed my palms over my ears in order to block out the noises outside. Then I got it. The barber had been so angry at my answer that he had stopped shaving my head. And so I became the prison joke.

On January 23, 1974, Amnon was declared missing. No one officially informed us that he was imprisoned in Syria. The media rumors that no more prisoners remained there did not remove the doubt that rankled within us. But on the other hand, the news about the advanced contact with Egypt and the talk of an exchange of prisoners in that country encouraged us to explore all avenues.

We participated in the activities of the Committee of Families of MIAs *and Prisoners of the Syrian Front. They enlisted international public opinion and contacted world organizations, asking them to lobby their governments. The governments should pressure Syria to release the list of prisoners, allow visits of Red Cross representatives, and free the prisoners. The committee held meetings and discussions with Prime Minister Golda Meir, Minister of Defense Moshe Dayan, Vice President Yigal Allon, and the chairman of the Knesset Foreign Affairs and Security Committee, Knesset member Haim Zadok.*

In addition, we decided that for the good of our loved ones, we would refrain from outspoken activities in Israel. This was "to prevent our enemies from torturing our children and avoid raising the price we will have to pay in order to redeem our prisoners."

February. Time crawled sluggishly. In between the interrogations, the meals and the prayers, I lay alone in my cell, staring at the ceiling and thinking about Bella and the advancing pregnancy. How was she? She was in the seventh month already. What would she name the baby? What was happening in my publishing firm? Who was working on the *Address Book for Commerce and Industry in Israel*, in which I had invested three years of work and had just finished before Yom Kippur? On Friday, Yom Kippur Eve, I had left everything in the office, as I did every other day.

My gaze slipped from the ceiling to the stained walls, and my eyes darted across them as if reading an open book. My eyelids grew heavy and began to droop. The stains on the wall grew blurry and transformed into images of people.

They're taking me out of the cell through the hole in the plywood that covers the high window facing the outside. Secretly, they smuggle me out of the prison. Under cover of darkness, they put me in a cart hitched to a horse, place packages of rags over me and take me to a cave in the region of the Al-Hamah hills, near the Israel-Syria border. There

members of the Jewish community in Damascus welcome
me. They are waiting for the opportunity to transfer me
to the other side of the border. The cave is dark and deep,
and for a few days we eat rations that someone smuggles
us from the prison.

One night, they wake me up and whisper to me in
Arabic-accented Hebrew: "It's time." I rub my eyes, and by
the light of a small flashlight crawl to the cave entrance. We
advance, bent to the ground. The dawn rises, and the sky
is reflected in the Kinneret like a work of art. From among
the trees, out bursts my family. They move toward me with
hesitation, but I widen my steps, spread my arms, and glide
toward them, light as a bird. I land straight in the arms of
my wife, Bella. Slowly my parents come toward us, and my
sister and Bella's parents, and in our giant embrace we are
like an old, thick tree trunk that time cannot weather. "Dad,
I'm here, too!" says little Raviv, pulling at my shirt. I grab his
narrow waist, lift him up and clutch him to my chest. We
stand together, full of emotion, and the tears stream from
our eyes into a small puddle underneath us.

When I woke up, the blanket under my head was soaked with
tears and my eyes stung.

After lunch they took me for interrogation. They asked me
about the structure of the tank brigade, and because I really didn't
know all the details, I said that the tank brigade had three battalions.

"And what else is in the brigade?"

"I'm only a company commander and I don't know what else
is in the brigade. I barely know what's in the battalion, but I know
the company well," I said, acting like an expert.

As expected, my answers were insufficient. I suffered mighty
blows to my neck, and punches rained down on my shoulders like
hammers. "I remember!" I screamed in pain, trying to revoke the
punishment. "The brigade also has a mortar company, a commu-

nications company, and…" No one was interested. They continued beating me, running amok, and the more I shouted, the more they beat me. Suddenly the blows stopped, and the soldier who had been beating my back now flicked a wooden toothpick along it. This was more unendurable than the beatings, and I almost lost my senses.

After they brought me back to my cell, beaten and bleeding, I sterilized the wounds with the orange-peel essence I had saved for times of trouble. As I was tending to my wounds, the door opened again and they took me for another interrogation.

"Tell us about the night stops of the armored corps," one of the investigators began.

"We always drive at night. We don't stop." I tried to avoid giving information, but again I only succeeded in annoying the interrogator. He screamed and raged, and someone beat my face with a rubber hose. My lips tore, and I tried to stop the blood with my tongue.

"How do you make night stops?" the interrogator insisted. I said I didn't know what he meant. They sat me next to the table, removed the black sack, handed me a pencil and paper and demanded that I draw a night stop of a tank company. I remembered that once, in a class on tank battle theory, the instructor had made a circle of tanks with the barrels pointing out, and I drew a picture of that.

This seemed to calm the seas slightly. One of the interrogators approached me, and in a calm and polite tone, he addressed me in Hebrew. "Look, Amnon, I only want what's good for you. It's worth it for you to cooperate with us. In the end we'll give you a new wife, a house in a village somewhere in Syria and a donkey, and you'll have a good life." His generous offer moved me; some people here were humane after all. I thanked him but refused his offer politely. "I have a pregnant wife and a little boy at home, and my home is in Israel, not in Syria," I explained.

When I returned to the cell, I memorized the drawing of the night stop, so that if they asked me again, I would know how to draw it exactly.

The coming interrogations also focused on military topics. "Eagle Eyes" began one interrogation by asking, "What does the reconnaissance company do in the brigade?"

"As far as I know, there aren't any reconnaissance companies in the tank brigade, only in the infantry brigades. I'm not familiar with the infantry brigades at all," I replied, and as usual...

"You're lying! You're bluffing! You're telling tales!" And two brutes with sharpened sticks in their hands attacked me from behind. They stabbed my back, my thighs and the back of my neck. They cut me like a steak before it goes on the grill, and I felt my body ripping.

"God, they're killing me!" I shouted to Heaven. The interrogator shouted back, "Answer me! You know the answer! You're lying!!" A sharpened skewer pierced my tailbone, and sharp pain cleaved my backbone. I swayed in place, and suddenly found myself on the floor, the torn soles of my feet in the air. The rubber rod sliced the air, whipping them with the horrifying *falak* beatings.

I awoke in my solitary cell, soaked to the bones. I could not bring myself to eat the spinach leaves from dinner. I felt severe nausea and weakness, as if I were gradually retreating from my body. I parted from Bella and wished her an easy birth. I don't know how long I lay that way, but I woke up to the sound of screams and shouts erupting from one of the cells. I felt my body to make sure I was alive. If they had not managed to get rid of me by then, I thought, they would certainly succeed in the tortures to come. I lay there until morning, worn out and tense. I listened to the sounds from the corridor and the screams from the adjacent cells, in the horrible anticipation that any moment, the door would open and I would return to hell.

In the morning, as usual, they took me to the latrine. The guard pulled the sack down around my head. As he dragged me through the corridor like a beast to the slaughter, he banged my head on the walls, first to the right, then to the left.

After that they served breakfast: an orange plate full of the usual wormy tea, two *hubez* breads one on top of the other, and white cheese on top. That was the first time I had eaten white cheese since I had left home. It was bright white and smooth, and looked amazingly fresh. I licked my swollen, cracked lips in anticipation and dipped my tongue into the soft cheese. Yuck! My face contorted in disgust. The cheese was sour. I was convinced they were trying to poison me, and spat until I felt safe.

Soon the guard came into the cell to take out the empty plate. When he saw that I hadn't eaten the cheese, his face expressed surprise. I explained to him in pantomime that my stomach hurt and if he wanted, he could eat it. He looked behind himself to the corridor, looked back at me, placed his finger over his lips and whispered, "Shhh." I nodded my head and I also placed my finger on my mouth in collaboration. Then he put his fingers into the cheese and licked them in delight, until not a trace remained. When he was finished, he wiped his mouth and moustache carefully, made me swear not to tell, and left the cell.

The whole day I watched him, and when I saw that nothing bad happened to him, I decided that next time, I would eat the white cheese. And so, a few days later they gave me white cheese again, and even though it was very sour, I ate and enjoyed it…and ever since, I have liked *labaneh* ever since.

Toward evening I heard the thunder of cannons not far off. Could it be that the IDF had reached Damascus? I wondered. The reverberations of the explosions took me back to my compulsory service, when I was a company commander in Battalion 82. On one of the days before I was to be released, Gorodish (Shmuel Gonen), the commander of the 7th Brigade, called me to his quarters in Nafah and tried to convince me to sign up for career service. I explained to him that I had other plans and that I wasn't so interested in signing. He rose from his seat in annoyance and opened the window. With one hand he grasped my hand, and with the other, he gestured toward the north and said, "You see, Amnon, Damascus is over there. We're going out to conquer it, and you'll be at home, not with us!" I replied that although I was being discharged from regular service, I would be available for reserve duty any time.

As fate would have it, here I was the only one who got here, and Gorodish and all the rest stayed back in Israel. How I missed them. I prayed my third prayer for that day, and went to sleep in an improved mood, humming to myself my regular song: "Bye-bye, Monday; hello, Tuesday. I hope it'll be a good day, I hope it'll be a wonderful day…"

The next day was calm. I began to make friends with the "dancers" that squirmed from the cracks in the ceiling, and in my mind I drew the images of those who had written the Arabic graffiti on the walls. Too bad I don't know how to read Arabic, I thought to myself, and carved my name in Hebrew on the wall using the pin I had found in the pajamas. Later lunch arrived. The orange plastic plate was full of bean soup and half a tangerine. Enjoying the relative calm, I ate that soup as if it were the most delicious bean soup I had ever eaten in my life. For the dessert of this royal feast, I had the half tangerine. Then I squeezed the peel onto my scabbed wounds, encouraged that I was sterilizing them and healing my body.

After lunch, on a full stomach, I sprawled along the length of a stripe of light that penetrated through the crack in the wood covering the window. As I gazed at the light, I fell into a reverie, and again I saw the three Red Cross representatives who authorized my release on June 8. I imagined my return home, the emotional meeting with my family and my joy at the baby about to be born. During the hours when I was awake and alert, I invented games to exercise my mind, such as math problems, recalling the names of the Maccabi Tel Aviv basketball players, various dates, and so forth. The main thing was to prevent my brain from atrophying, to preserve my senses. On occasion, I would also try to stretch my body carefully and walk inside the narrow cell, but the soles of my feet were painful. The regular routine of interrogations, beatings and tortures did not even allow the wounds time to scab.

Having experienced the Auschwitz concentration camp, I know that a person can stand every kind of suffering, but there were moments when I almost broke. Until Amnon was declared missing, I did not understand the depth of the suffering felt by the prisoners' mothers and wives. Despite all our emotional strength, sometimes we neared the abyss. Half of February has passed, and we still have received no formal announcement about the prisoners. Amnon's business has been paralyzed since he left for the war. All our pleas for assistance have been in vain. The uncertainty is the most difficult of all. The media reported false rumors that all the prisoners were killed. People in the neighborhood and acquaintances were not optimistic either, saying that the Syrians were very cruel.

In one interrogation, again they asked me about the structure of a brigade and a division, and for the umpteenth time, I said I didn't know anything about them. As usual, I did not succeed in convincing the interrogators, and the beatings rained down, opening wounds that had just begun to scab. "When I get back to Israel, I'll enlist in the army and I'll learn what's in a brigade and a division," I screamed in desperation. A rubber hose cut my face, and one of my lower front teeth flew out of my mouth. My face burned under the black sack, and I felt streams of blood flowing from my cheeks and mouth. "We'll cut off your fingers and toes so you won't be able to serve in the army!" I heard the translator mutter near my ear. "Even if you take off my hands and feet, I'll join the army!" I informed him defiantly with the last of my strength, and fainted.

When I woke up in my cell, I was wet and gushing with blood. Why did I tell him I would join the army, I rebuked myself. I've never been interested in that, and I even told Gorodish that I would not sign up for career service. So why did I make trouble for myself? Revenge burned within me. I felt my body fill with new energy I had never felt before. I imagined how I would grab the interrogator who had tortured me and take him to a solitary house near the sand dunes of Bat Yam. The tortures I carried out on him in my mind gave me chills. Amnon, I said to myself, you shouldn't think about that, because maybe the Syrians will learn how to read your thoughts and do those same things to you.

Of all the dreams I had, three repeated themselves often: the dream about release on June 8, the one about the Merkavah tank, and the one of the bed and mattress factory. The imaginary world I created for myself helped me to maintain my sanity and preserve hope. It kept me busy with "people" I liked and with new ideas that seemed interesting and creative, at least in my dreams.

"Today is Friday, February 22," I repeated to myself as soon as I woke up, as if to convince myself that I had left the realm of dreams. In the corridor, the bustle was greater than usual. Heavy doors opened but did not close, objects were dragged, and cries in Arabic echoed between the walls. What was going on? Where was everyone going? What else would they do to me? I went out of my mind. The world was in a commotion around me, and I was here in my dark cell, isolated from all visual information, imagining scenes of horror in my head.

Toward evening the noises in the corridor ceased, and they took me to the latrine with my eyes covered. Suddenly I heard from a distance an indistinct echo in a language that was not Arabic. As I approached the latrine, the voices became clearer – it was powerful singing in Hebrew. They were singing Sabbath songs, songs that I knew. During dinner the singing continued, and it even accompanied my nighttime prayer. What was happening to me? Was I hearing voices and losing my mind? I pinched myself, and in order to banish the evil thoughts I began to do math problems in my head. But it was useless, the singing only grew stronger. I guess I'm hallucinating, I thought, and fell asleep in a deep depression.

The next day, Saturday, the guard named Bash came in. At least that is what I heard someone call him, and so I had decided to call him that name. Bash was a young man of average height with light hair, and his eyes flashed evil. When he came in with breakfast, I stood at attention with only my underwear on. He took the burning cigarette from his mouth and began to extinguish it on my chest. Round, red burns appeared on my skin, and with each burn I twisted my face in pain, but I did not open my mouth. When he finished the cigarette, he picked up a thin iron rod and lightly carved a word in Arabic on my chest. *"Kulo tayarin...*(all the pilots)," he said, and muttered a sentence in Arabic, drawing his finger across his neck while smiling at me. I understood that the singing I had heard was from the pilots, and concluded from the slaughter sign he made across his neck that they had been united together in one cell. I asked him, "And when do I go?" gesturing at my neck with my finger. Bash smiled at me, and he left the cell without a word. I ate breakfast, hoping that soon they would put me together with the pilots and end the oppressive isolation of the last five months.

> *My daughter Bella agreed to go with me to a family wedding. I thought this was a good way to give her a break from the tension that surrounds her. We called a taxi, and my husband stayed at home with Raviv. From the radio, the deep, serious voice of the announcer broadcast a special bulletin. "Please stop," I asked the driver. Terrible thoughts raced through my head. Outside, cars continued passing by, and droves of people walked among the stores in enjoyment. Cold sweat covered my face. Bella, who sat next to me in the back seat, looked at me in worry. She didn't understand what was happening to me. "All the prisoners in Syria have been murdered," the announcer declared. A black cloud covered my eyes. I hugged Bella, and in a shaking voice I whispered to the driver: "Take us home."*
>
> *After that I couldn't fall asleep at night. Every time I put my head on the pillow, I saw horrifying scenes. I felt helpless. I would not share my pain with anyone else, so as to preserve the delicate balance each member of the family had achieved. I even refused to take the tranquilizers the doctor gave me, because I had to function for everyone – cooking, taking care of Bella, giving the boy attention. I had to be awake and busy all the time. I could not allow myself to cry*

at home, I could not allow myself to cry in front of Raviv
and most certainly not in front of Bella – the only person I
could cry in front of was the psychologist.

Monday morning, the door opened. It wasn't time for a meal
or for the trip to the latrine, so I worried they were taking me for
interrogation again after the break of the last few days. Two jailers
I did not recognize stood in the opening of the cell. One of them
threw the black sack at me to put over my head, while the second
one picked up the mattress and the meager items I had accumulated. Pushing and berating me in Arabic, they led me in a new
direction to a flight of stairs. I climbed up carefully and stopped
before a doorway. When one of the guards announced our arrival,
the door opened, and they took the sack off and pushed me into
a large room. They threw in my mattress after me, along with the
blankets, the pajamas and the little towel.

IN PRISON WITH THE PILOTS

From behind wild manes of hair and untamed beards on sunken cheeks, pairs of eyes stared at me. At first glance, these gaunt prisoners looked like Arabs. Some wore pajamas, others only their underwear. Examining me from head to toe, they mumbled, "Nesher, Nesher." They've put me in a room together with Arabs, I thought, fearing for my life. Now they'll take their revenge. Then they began to approach me, ghostlike. Some walked on two feet, while others hopped on one foot, supported by their friends. Cold sweat covered my body and my brain began to work feverishly. From articles I had read in the newspapers, I knew that there was always at least one Damascus Jew in this prison. "Are there any Jews here?" I whispered in Hebrew. Then the prisoners said, disappointed, "Guys, it isn't Nesher!" (Ze'ev Nesher was a pilot who was supposedly in the Damascus hospital, and whose build was apparently similar to mine.) My heart lifted. These were air force crewmen, and it was their singing I had heard on Shabbat eve, making me think I was losing my mind.

The new room was enormous compared to the solitary confinement cell. It was about twenty-six feet (eight meters) wide and sixty-five feet (twenty meters) long. The ceiling was very high, and several light bulbs hung from it. The light switch was outside the cell, which meant we were dependent on the guards' mercies for light. The bathroom cubicle in the corner shielded a latrine and a faucet with a rubber hose attached to it. A small sink and faucet stood outside the compartment. Next to the sink was a cask of water, for emergencies when the faucet was dry. Shuttered windows ran low along the wall next to the door. Another row

of windows, also shuttered, lined the top of the narrow wall that
faced the outside.

We spread our mattresses on the cement floor alongside the
walls. In the middle of the room stood a kind of radiator, a tank
connected to a spherical metal container full of crude oil. From
this container, a tin pipe of about eight inches (twenty centimeters)
in diameter rose to the ceiling. We lit the radiator with a match,
then sat around it and warmed ourselves as if it were a bonfire. We
could also warm tea on it and toast the *hubez* bread.

After I had organized my belongings, I introduced myself to
my new friends. They were twenty in number, all air force crew:
pilots and navigators, some in the reserves and some in the standing army.

Shortly afterward, three new men joined us. The first was a
tank captain who was a company commander from Battalion 82.
Next to enter was the doctor on Mt. Hermon, a reservist of about
forty who was the "old man" in the group, and the third was the
Hermon intelligence officer. As soon as the intelligence officer came
in, he sat down, held his head in his hands and murmured in tears,
"The damage I've done to the State of Israel! It will take them the
next twenty years to put it right…" We placated him, saying we
had all done damage of one kind or another, but that the state was
strong enough to get over it.

The room was packed. After we had all arranged our mattresses
and meager possessions, we all sat cross-legged around the radiator, a group of rail-thin men sporting black beards. In a spontane-
ous initiative, each one of us began in turn to tell about himself.
We talked about our families and military background. Then we
each recounted our battle story, how we were taken captive, and
our experiences in solitary confinement.

In the afternoon, the door opened. We stood at attention, and
the guards brought in large tin containers full of rice, a box full
of apples, a pile of plastic plates and metal spoons. We divided up
the food. Everyone received a heaping portion, and we ate our fill,
sitting around the radiator. After that we washed the dishes and

returned to sit around the radiator and recount our personal stories.

"Let's run a lottery," suggested one of the men. "Whoever makes the closest guess for the date of our release wins a free meal in the fanciest restaurant we choose." Each one put in his guess. Some thought a week, others guessed another month or two. The pessimists among us said a full year. When my turn came, I said with complete assurance, "We're going home on June 8th." Silence fell in the room and the eyes of my comrades opened wide in astonishment. "June 8th??" One of the pilots broke the silence. "Explain and justify your answer."

This was the first time in my life I had ever met pilots. I had heard fascinating stories and tales of bravery about them, and to me they were an exalted race. "There's nothing to explain. That's my date in the lottery and that's it," I mumbled, embarrassed to tell them about my dream.

"You know, I was wounded in December. A month before that, there was an exchange of prisoners with Egypt after extensive negotiations," one of the pilots recounted, trying to cheer us up.

"I know!" I said to the young man sitting next to me as I smiled to myself. This time I couldn't get out of the explanation, and I told them my dream about the meeting with the Red Cross and the announcement that we would go home on June 8th.

The first day with my new friends ended. I recited my prayer, and added the plea that the days to come should not get any worse. For the first time in many months, I fell asleep with the secure feeling that I was not alone.

Dawn rose and the men woke up. We lined up for the latrine, then got organized until breakfast came: a can full of sweet tea, a sack of *hubez* bread and a dish of olives. We sat around the radiator and divided up the food. As we ate, we talked and joked. I made friends with Meir, a Phantom jet pilot. He taught me about the Phantom, and I taught him about tanks.

In the afternoon hours, the jailers gave out masks to cover our eyes, and we went down in a line to the group showers, which had no dividers between them. Two days passed without disturbances or interrogations, and we had the chance to deepen our acquaintances and prepare ourselves for the days ahead.

February 27. We received a message that US Secretary of State Henry Kissinger would arrive with a list of prisoners. Moshe, Amnon's father, sped to the Kiryah (Israel's Pentagon), and I waited along with my mother-in-law at home. We had anticipated this day for four months. Finally it had arrived, but I was not ready for it. I was afraid. I wanted to put it off for a few days, so that I could hope some more, so that I wouldn't have to face a final ending if, God forbid, he wasn't on the list.

The parents of the prisoners gathered at the Kiryah, and at 4:00 P.M. we received a message that Kissinger had brought the list. The room was packed wall to wall. When the representative of the Ministry of Defense came in, complete silence reigned. He began to read the names in alphabetical order. My body began to shake, and a cold sweat broke out on my face. "Sharon, Amnon" was one of the last names he read.

Until that February 27, I had held on. I had to be strong and not neglect myself. But on the day the list arrived, I was afraid that if he wasn't on it, I would not be able to take the disappointment. I decided to wait at home with Bella. In the late afternoon, the telephone rang. I was petrified to pick it up, and Bella also hesitated. She was in the seventh month of pregnancy already, and we didn't know how she would react if, God forbid… I hurried over to the neighbor and asked, "Can you please pick up the phone and listen to what he says?" She trembled with fear as she held the receiver, and in a shaking voice whispered, "Moshe?" I put my palms together and murmured to myself, "If only,

if only…" "Yes! Yes!" she shouted, and in a few minutes the
house filled with neighbors who came to rejoice with us
and encourage us.

During that time the Syrians eased up on us slightly. We
sensed that they were making special preparations. On March 1,
1974, they informed us that the Red Cross was coming to visit. They
instructed us to put on the Syrian uniforms they had handed out.
After breakfast, three men entered the room. It was just as I had
seen in my dream, except they were not plump at all, but rather
thin, pale Swiss, with eyeglasses on their noses and Red Cross
badges on their clothes. We asked the Syrian officers to leave the
room and tried to talk to the Swiss. The information they gave us
was sparse. "We are walking on eggs. We don't want to risk an-
gering the Syrians," they said. They gave us postcards on which
we were allowed to write only our personal details and as many
words as would fit on one line. Below were boxes to check, marked
"wounded," "healthy," "ill," and so forth. At the end of the visit they
read us telegrams from home: congratulations to one on his birthday, to another for a new baby daughter and for a third, a baby boy.
I did not receive any messages, so I assumed that Bella had not yet
given birth and everything was fine.

The list Kissinger brought had confirmed that Amnon was
alive in the Syrian prison, but his condition remained a
question until we received the official message from the
chief adjutant on March 4, 1974:

Dear Family,
Following our letter of Wednesday, February 27, 1974,
that your loved one is on the list of Israeli prisoners in Syria,
we are pleased to inform you that the representative of the
International Red Cross visited our prisoners in Syria on
Friday, March 1, 1974, and found your family member in
good physical and emotional condition.

Your family member asked the International Red Cross
representative to send you his greetings as well as this pris-
oner card, written in his own handwriting. We will inform
you as soon as we receive any additional details.
    Cordially yours,
      The Chief Adjutant

Our room was very crowded. Twenty-four mattresses were
spread along the walls. Next to each mattress, we placed our sparse
personal belongings: blankets, a small towel, a Syrian uniform, and
pajamas. Three times a day they would bring us the meals, and we
began to get organized for an extended stay.

Some of the pilots were amputees, but they functioned like
everyone else. I still thought of pilots as special people, and the
behavior of these officers only increased my admiration for them.
They would hop from place to place on one leg, and insisted on
taking their turns in all the chores. For example, one man's leg was
amputated to the knee. We offered to relieve him of his turn to
wash the dishes, but he refused, and found a method of standing
next to the sink for a long time. He would stick his stump in the
metal ring on the hot water cask next to the sink, and that way he
could wash the dishes like the rest of us. Eventually, the amputees
made themselves crutches from the wooden fruit crates. To make
it easier for them to use the bathroom, they built a special wooden
seat to use over the latrine.

Miki, who spoke excellent English, volunteered to teach us.
Every day we would gather together at an appointed time to learn
new words and sing songs in English. Slowly, we even began to
converse in the language. Amos, the Hermon intelligence officer,
spoke fluent Arabic, and he developed his own course in which
he taught us words, sentences and even expressions. Gabi Gerzon
was a very talented artist and drew us in caricature, using a small
piece of red pencil that came our way. For the paper we used for
drawing and in our activities, we scrounged from what the Syrians brought us. For example, we used the wrappings of the bread

and the other food to write on. In addition, we saved white sheets that we ripped out of English propaganda books, the only written material we had at that point.

In addition to studies, we also manufactured our own games. At meals we received triangles of soft cheese from Holland. We peeled off their colorful wrappers, and Gabi drew the shapes of the card deck on them. Louie the doctor could play bridge and taught us his bag of tricks. We would sit for hours in groups of four and pass the time. Whoever tired of cards could play chess or backgammon. We drew a checkered playing board on one of the mattresses, and used playing pieces carved from soap. Later, packages from Israel arrived with real board games, jackstraws, and various types of cards, enough for all of us.

Aside from board games, we also amused ourselves with pantomime, musical chairs, and many other games we used to play in our youth groups. We did macramé and made "jewelry" out of olive pits and recycled materials.

Life in the big room operated like a commune. We appointed a committee that was responsible for a daily schedule, and that also served as our representatives to the Syrians. The food committee had two members, and its job was to organize the meals and set aside food for special occasions. The sports committee organized physical activities, such as obstacle courses between the mattresses and exercises. Together with the food committee, the cultural committee planned the holidays and *Kabbalat Shabbat*. The cultural committee also arranged "movie nights," which we awaited impatiently. Once a week, according to the order of the beds, one of us would recount the plot of a film he had seen. If he couldn't remember a film, he had to make one up. We sat glued to our seats, like in a real movie theater, as the storyteller tried his best to make his story come alive.

Every Friday evening we held a *Kabbalat Shabbat* service. For wicks, we used strands of wool pulled from blankets and mattresses. We dipped them in oil gathered from the bottoms of the rice containers. We placed these "candles" on pieces of cardboard that served as candleholders, and the religious among us recited the blessing. The food committee prepared a Shabbat meal, which included a cocktail made of fruit saved from what we received during the week. After the meal, we would sing songs and try to maintain the special atmosphere of Shabbat as much as possible.

Purim was especially amusing. "Hey ho, we are a wall / And on our lips is a single call / Nothing can scare us / Nothing can scare us / Hey ho, we are a wall…" Our voices joined in a powerful three-part harmony Gabi taught us. Our singing shook the bare walls of the room, summoning the guards, who ran to our room to check on the prisoners who had gone berserk. They burst inside like in a military operation, and we greeted them with, "*Hag Purim, hag Purim, hag gadol la-yeladim* (Purim holiday, Purim holiday, a wonderful holiday for children)." We sang like a bunch of idiots. The guards stopped in the middle of the room. After recovering from their shock, they smiled to each other as if to say, "Poor things, they've gone out of their minds." Then they left us alone. We hadn't laughed and acted so silly in a long time. We recalled childhood tunes, told jokes, and performed skits. We felt that truly, nothing could scare us as long as "Hey ho, we are a wall."

The Hebrew calendar includes a wide spectrum of holidays and events that connect individual Jews with the land as well as with their fellow Jews. Each and every day of our long stay in prison, we felt this elemental truth in our flesh. The Purim celebration left us feeling uplifted, and we decided to prepare for Passover well in advance. Because our group included individuals from secular kibbutzim as well as from traditional backgrounds, we had discussions about the nature of the holiday and how to observe it. Should we observe it according to Jewish law, or as a celebration of spring, as the kibbutz members do? Finally, we decided to keep Seder night according to Jewish law, because we were in exile and this was the best way to feel close to Israel and home. The second holiday we would observe as a celebration of spring.

Amos and Gili, our religion "experts," reconstructed the Haggadah. As before the war I had owned a publishing house, and was also gifted with graphic talents, I took the role of writing out the Haggadah on small pieces of paper. I even copied it several times by hand. We also prepared "matzos" in advance by saving pieces of toast, since the Syrians refused to provide us with proper matzos.

One day at the end of March, the door opened and the guards brought in boxes full of towels and T-shirts. "Packages from Israel!" cried one of the men, seeing the Hebrew print on the shirts. Our excitement knew no bounds. Finally a material connection with Israel – the Israeli government was not neglecting us! Throughout the day they brought more and more boxes, until our room looked like a warehouse: books, games, toothpaste and toothbrushes, battery-operated shavers, and…supplies for Passover, including matzos and Haggadahs.

Around the world on April Fools' Day, April 1, people tell tall tales and play tricks on each other, trying to avoid getting caught. Early in the morning of April 1, 1974, the guards opened the door to our room, brought in our breakfast – and left the door open. Were they making fun of us? Maybe they were looking for an excuse to torture us again if we tried to run outside or even just take a peek? But no, it was for real. The Syrians surprised us and invited us to go out onto the large balcony outside the room. On occasion we had heard Syrian prisoners walking around there, and through the cracks in the shutters we could see them walking along the large walls to which stone sinks and faucets were attached. We went outside and blinked our eyes under the clear blue sky. The warm sun caressed our faces, reminding us that a world awaited us outside the prison. For six months I had seen neither sky nor sunlight, so I felt very inspired. I breathed lungfuls of fresh air as if hoarding stock for the coming days, and walked back and forth, praying that the jailers would also enjoy the break outside for a while.

Like all good things, those moments of mercy came to an end earlier than desired. But the surprises for that day were not yet over. The Red Cross representatives came for their second visit. They gave us an itemized list of the materials that had been sent from Israel, including clothes, toiletries, canned goods, books, games, and religious objects. They also brought letters. We felt wonderful. The Hebrew writing on the products reminded us of home, and we no longer felt isolated. I received new clothes and cloth shoes, and finally I could walk around in sweatpants and a T-shirt instead of underwear. I could put my wounded feet into soft shoes instead of on the cold, rough floor. The shaver and toiletries made us look like civilized men once again. Daily activities we considered chores at home, such as shaving or brushing our teeth, took on new value in prison. After growing a thick beard for six months, there was nothing more pleasant in the world than to feel my face smooth once again. There was no greater enjoyment than to massage my teeth and gums with fresh toothpaste, the taste of which I had sorely missed.

Among the books that arrived were volumes of the Tanakh (Hebrew Scriptures) signed by the IDF rabbi. Even for the secular Jews among us, these gifts were much appreciated. The guards kept the canned goods so they could check that nothing had been smuggled inside them. But since we had the lists, we knew exactly what had arrived. At mealtime we could order whatever we wanted, just like in a restaurant. Hummus, meat, vegetable loaf, and halva were some of the options. The moment the packages began to arrive from Israel, everything became easier and more pleasant. Even the guards' treatment of us improved immeasurably.

At the end of the visit, the Red Cross representatives read out telegrams from home: congratulations on your birthday, or for the birth of a baby boy or girl. My heart began to pound – they're going to tell me that I had a baby as well. We rejoiced for each other, as if each baby that came into the world was a victory for us all. When they did not call out my name, I was very anxious. According to my calculations, Bella should have given birth by now. I was certain she had miscarried and they didn't want to worry me. On second thought, I encouraged myself, miscarriages do not happen so easily. Perhaps she had simply given birth after the Red Cross representatives had left for Syria? Amnon, think positive, I repeated to myself, morning and evening. Thanks to your emotional strength, you've hung on until now. You'll see, everything will be all right. But my doubts lingered. I waited impatiently for the letters from home, but in them…not a word about the birth.

At the end of the Red Cross visits, each one of us would go into his own corner and withdraw into himself. Some faces shone with smiles, while others concealed tears of emotion. Silence enveloped the room, and sorrow mingled with longing and anticipation for the next batch of letters swept over us all.

The days passed and Passover approached. Together we scrubbed the room, cleaning and polishing. We prepared the dishes and arranged the mattresses to form a rectangular table in the center. On the eve of the holiday we bathed ourselves in the bathroom faucet, put on the new clothes we had received from home and sat around our makeshift Seder table. Louie, the oldest among us, sat at the head of the table and conducted the Seder along with Amos, the group "rabbi." Gili, the youngest, asked the Four Questions. We read from the Haggadahs that had arrived from Israel shortly before the holiday, and we recited the blessing over the "wine" – coffee diluted with water. We danced and sang, and the rejoicing lasted until the early hours of the morning.

That Passover in exile in an enemy prison took on special significance. We were prisoners just as our forefathers had been, except instead of in Egypt, we were in Syria. Just as they had hoped and prayed to go out from slavery into freedom, so did we.

The intermediate days of Passover, Hol Ha-Mo'ed, passed pleasantly. For the second holiday, we again arranged the mattresses in the center of the room and read a humorous Haggadah we had written ourselves. We sang songs about spring and gave our regular guards names of characters from the Haggadah. At the end, we sang the traditional concluding song, praying that this year, we would all arrive in a rebuilt Jerusalem.

Sunday, April 7, Seder night. This was one of the saddest days I had experienced in the last few months. The entire family sat around the holiday table in their finest clothes.

Little Raviv sat next to his grandfather, waiting with excite-ment to sing the Four Questions for the first time. Before reading the Haggadah, we all rose to our feet for a moment of silence. We offered a prayer for Amnon's speedy return. Our eyes turned longingly to the picture placed on the table next to his chair, which stood empty as if awaiting a mira-cle. We performed the Seder according to the law and ate the holiday dishes, but inside us, a bitter taste remained – Amnon was still gone.

Wednesday, April 10, the third day of Hol Ha-Mo'ed. That day I missed Amnon more than anything. I missed the loving caress on my way to the hospital. I missed the firm pressure of his hand at the moment of birth, and more than anything, his calming presence. In the morning, the contrac-tions began, and I went to the hospital with my father-in-law. Although it was Passover, spring had yet to arrive. The sky was gray, and rain darkened our moods. The birth went smoothly. A boy was born, sweet and calm. We named him Dror ("freedom"). The hospital staff treated me like a queen. I got a private room. Tel Aviv Mayor "Cheech" (Shlomo) Lahat and Simcha Holzberg, spokesman for the wounded, came to visit me. From dawn till dusk, friends and family came to offer their support and share in my happiness. But as I watched the other women sitting on their beds with their husbands and children, I felt sadness mixed with a tinge of jealousy. I could only hope that soon I would be able to do the same.

Holocaust Memorial Day arrived. We were not completely certain of its date, but we knew that it fell somewhere between Passover and Yom Ha-Atzma'ut. We held a ceremony, lighting a memorial candle and reciting the *Yizkor* memorial prayer. Then Guri, a Phantom navigator, organized a somber discussion on the topic of the Holocaust. How had the Holocaust influenced the founding of the state? Could the Holocaust happen again? How should we educate our children to remember it, and thus to act with bravery in future wars? These were topics that Israelis always discussed, in school and in the army, but never before had they been so relevant.

About a week later, we observed Yom Ha-Zikaron, Israel's Memorial Day for fallen IDF soldiers, and Yom Ha-Atzma'ut, Independence Day. Using the meager means at our disposal, we drew the Israeli flag on a T-shirt and raised it on a makeshift pole made from the leg of a bed. Then we lowered it to half-mast. An honor guard stood beside it, and we all saluted for two minutes of silence. We also lit a candle in memory of the fallen. This year, many of our friends were among them. We read the *Yizkor* memorial prayer and sang appropriate songs, quiet and melancholy.

This day of remembrance was overwhelming for us, although we were young officers whose physical and emotional strength had enabled us to hold up under severe torture in an enemy prison. We shed tears as we recalled the fallen soldiers, for there but for the grace of God were we, and the threat that we might join them still hung over us.

To conclude Yom Ha-Zikaron, we again stood at attention for two minutes before the partially lowered flag. Then we raised it to the top of the pole, ate a festive dinner and began activities for Yom Ha-Atzma'ut. Two by two, we lit torches, and each couple said a few words they had prepared in honor of the event. I lit a torch together with Danny, the other tanker. We addressed our speech to the armored corps: "On the twenty-sixth Independence Day of the State of Israel, we hereby light this torch in memory of the fighters of the armored corps who met their deaths in Israel's battles. We honor the armored corps and its brave soldiers who are constantly prepared for action and whose cannons threaten Damascus. We salute the wounded in Israel and abroad, the soldiers of the IDF, and the glory of the State of Israel."

We stayed up until dawn singing songs about Israel, telling battle stories and tales of heroism, and hoping that we would celebrate the next Yom Ha-Atzma'ut in Israel, together with our loved ones.

On April 23, a guard entered the room with two Syrian prisoners and began to take apart the radiator. Until then, the radiator had served us as a social center. We would sit around it and chat, toast slices of bread, and warm tea on its chimney. Its removal represented a serious deterioration of conditions. We decided to demand they return it to us, but each time we asked the jailers, they answered us with "*bukrah*" – tomorrow. Tomorrow would come, but no radiator.

We had heated discussions about what to do. Some proposed that we threaten a hunger strike, while opponents argued that it was not a good idea to anger the Syrians. Finally, we announced to the guards that we refused to eat until they returned the radiator. After a short time, no less than the prison commandant presented himself in our room. We explained the problem to him, and he apologized and said that according to regulations, they had to remove the radiators from the cells in the summer. He promised that the matter would be arranged as soon as possible. To our amazement, that very same day they brought us a kerosene primus stove, and we had to make do with that. As part of the preparations for summer, they also switched our winter clothes for lighter, summer wear. Once every two weeks they would take us down to the shower, and once a month the barber shaved our heads. Every once in a while we even earned a short walk on the balcony. In addition, they brought us bunk beds, which made the room quite spacious.

The holidays ended, as did the transition from winter to summer equipment. The jailers left us to our business. We continued with our regular activities, such as macramé class. We made needles from the thin bones of the chicken we ate for dinner, and used them to make necklaces out of olive pits. For decoration, we added pompoms made from threads pulled out of the blankets and towels.

Under the leadership of Gabi, who was an excellent illustrator, we also made a wall mural for our writing and drawings. One day, Gabi drew the armor officers, Danny and me, pushing a tank whose barrel was hanging down. We hung up this drawing on the mural, and it attracted the attention of the guard. "What's this?" asked the guard in Arabic. "The war is over, that's why the barrel is hanging and we're pushing it into storage," I answered back clearly in Arabic. The guard smiled and left the room.

On Tuesdays we held a bridge tournament, and then continued with the movie tradition. The creations we came up with for this activity would have put the greatest filmmakers to shame.

I had made friends with Meir, the Phantom pilot, during that first meeting in the new room. He taught me the secrets of flight and I taught him about the structure of the tank. I invested a great deal of time in learning about the Phantom. I practiced the details and even prepared for weekly tests that Meir gave me. I became an "expert" in flying the Phantom, and Meir proposed that when we crossed the border back into Israel, I should approach the air force commander right away and ask to fly in a Phantom. I promised him I would – the very thought thrilled me.

May 1. We had just woken up, and before we had time to get organized, the Red Cross representatives surprised us with a visit. We got dressed quickly and sat down to write postcards home. Meanwhile, they gave us lists of the food items that had been deposited at the prison for us and read telegrams from Israel out loud. "Itamar Barnea, congratulations, you have a baby girl. Her name is

Lilach." I took a deep breath, hoping that this time I would not be disappointed, and I looked at the man with pleading eyes. Slowly he turned over the page and continued. "Next in line is a boy. Congratulations, a baby boy for…Amnon Sharon."

"It can't be," I protested. "It must be a mistake. Check again. My first child is a boy – his name is Raviv. The second one should be a girl."

He studied the lists again, clicked his tongue, and with an apologetic smile announced, "There's no mistake. It's a boy." After the Red Cross representatives left, I gathered the group together. We filled glasses of water, drank a *l'chaim* and made a public announcement: "I don't know what they're thinking of at home, but I'm calling the new baby Dror!"

> *Restrain your voice from weeping and your eyes from tears; for there is reward for your accomplishment – the word of Hashem – and they will return from the enemy's land. There is hope for your future – the word of Hashem – and your children will return to their border. (Jeremiah 31:15–16)*

Dear Bella,

> *Today I received the joyous news about the birth of the third man in our family. I'm proud of you. I hope you are all healthy. I imagine it is difficult for you, but at the same time I hope you are managing. Naturally, I thought of the name Dror and I am very, very happy.*
>
> *Many warm kisses to all of you,*
> *Amnon*

My dear, beloved son Dror,

> *Your name has a great deal of significance, Dror. Accept my blessings, and be at least as nice as your older brother Raviv. I pray that you will merit a good and happy life. (Wait until you meet me.) I have two pieces of advice for you: "Hear my son, the discipline of your father, and do*

not forsake the teaching of your mother. For they are an adornment of grace for your head" (Proverbs 1:8–9). My second piece of advice: always remember, "To make your ears attentive to wisdom, incline your heart to understanding" (Proverbs 2:2).

Yours lovingly,
Dad

My darling Raviv,

I hope you are healthy. You are probably very happy about the new baby. I miss you very much and love you very, very much. Now you are the big man in the house. You must take care of Mom and help her, and of course watch over your brother Dror very carefully. Remember that I am always guarding you.

Lots and lots of kisses,
Your father, Amnon

I signed my name on the note to Raviv, for I could not know whether I would ever see him again, and I wanted to be sure he would remember it.

A few days after the Red Cross visit, an important delegation of Syrians visited us, accompanied by doctors. One doctor checked our teeth with a pocket flashlight, while another one went around and asked us if we had any problems. They all poked, prodded and checked, but they didn't tell us anything.

"Apparently we're going home soon," said one of our group, trying to guess the reason for the surprise visit.

"Actually, I think that if they're checking us, we'll be staying here for a while longer," said another. Avi Barber, who always attempted to keep our mood buoyant, added in a serious tone, "And I think if polite Louie is hiccupping, it's a sign that we're sure to be released." We all laughed. Every evening, I had been repeating to myself the date in the dream, and I decided, "Guys, June 8th is approaching, and these are part of the preparations for going home."

The days passed devoid of special events. We mended our clothes, laundered, cleaned the room, and took turns reading the Bible, which was as in demand as a best-seller. When there was no news, one of us would let out a sigh, despairing that we would never get out of here. We sank into depression, thinking of the families we had left behind in Israel, our parents, wives, and the newborn children whom we had never met.

The relationships between roommates were positive, and friendships deepened. Although most men do not usually have heart-to-heart talks, in this familial setting we knew almost everything about everybody. With time, we began to suspect that Amos was spilling superfluous information to the Syrians. Unfortunately, we had to be careful not to talk next to him.

Amos Levinberg was an intelligence officer who was captured at the Hermon post at the beginning of the war. During his stay with us, we noticed that he had an amazing memory. His head stored a huge amount of information, and apparently the Syrians had discovered this as well, and were using their unique methods to pry it out of him. They told him that the State of Israel had been destroyed, and that they were establishing a "commemorative museum" based on their intelligence. When they caught him, they asked him to supply them with material for this project. To permit him to write without disturbance, they took him to an isolated villa, where they supervised his writing. After he had finished, they put him into the prison cell with us.

One day the jailers came and with no advance notice they took Danny the tanker away. All my fears of the unknown returned to me. What did they take him for? They had not interrogated us for a long time – what had happened now? Would they call me as well? Torture me again? What else do they want to know? The tension was nerve-racking. I paced from one side of the room to the other, tense, shaking with fright. I was sure that when they brought Danny back, they would take me. Danny returned completely white. "They interrogated me about the operation the tank force carried out on the Hermon," he reported. "From their questions, I understood that they caught more prisoners just recently. Apparently they were trying to verify information they received from those prisoners." When I asked if they had beaten him, he replied in the negative. I served him a cup of tea to calm him down, and when he finished drinking he went to sleep. I sat next to the sleeping Danny and studied his face, which wore a more peaceful expression than before. But as the rate of his breathing slowed, I felt the rate of my heartbeats pick up.

They're coming. My body tensed at the sound of brisk strides in the corridor. The door of the room opened a crack and the guard peeked inside. His eyes surveyed everyone, then rested on me. I sat hunched, hugging my knees with my arms, trying to shrink and become invisible.

"Amos," the guard signaled with his hand, and I continued to sit motionless as Amos left the room, awaiting the next developments.

I do not know how much time passed. Tense silence filled the room. The men tried to sleep, but in vain. Suddenly the grating of the lock split the silence, and Amos entered with a crooked smile on his face.

"What did they do to you?" I jumped on him.

"They interrogated me and beat me on the back," he answered in a whiny voice.

I did not believe a word he was saying. I tore off his pajama shirt, and as I had suspected, his back was smooth and unmarked.

"Liar!" I attacked him, screaming with all my might, taking out all my accumulated tension on him. If Noah hadn't jumped on me with his one leg and tried to calm me down with a glass of water, I would have torn Amos to shreds.

In May, as in April, a few events broke our routine. On most days, though, when nothing special happened, we were busy with our regular activities. First Amos would wake up for the morning prayers. When he had finished, we would eat breakfast, straighten the room, and begin our classes. Then we would get some exercise by running around the mattresses. Lunch followed a short break, and then we took a good rest. After that we had afternoon tea, played the board games we had received from Israel, and read. We ate dinner, and continued with our classes until bedtime.

May 10. Lag Ba-Omer. This holiday does not have religious meaning, like Passover, or national significance, like Yom Ha-Atzma'ut. But someone who is far from home in an enemy country will grasp at any reminder of his past. Unfortunately, the radiator that had served as our group bonfire was long gone, so to celebrate Lag Ba-Omer we were left with the boiled potatoes in their jackets that we received for dinner. As prizes for the games we organized, the food committee allotted us chocolate bars.

In mid-May, a new guy joined us, Assael. He wobbled in on a primitive prosthesis, and before we even managed to greet him, Meir grabbed him in a hug. It turned out that Assael had been in the same crew as Meir. Ever since they had abandoned their airplane, they had no idea what had happened to him. When the rest of us repeated the round of introductions we had made on our first night in the shared cell, he told us his story. Before long he befriended us and became like one of the old-timers.

May 19. Jerusalem Day – another excuse for a party. This day, like Yom Ha-Atzma'ut, had great significance for the "veterans" among us who had fought in the Six-Day War. The atmosphere was festive. We sang songs about Jerusalem and paid tribute to the city as our eternal capital. We told stories and organized a treasure hunt. One of us composed a brainteaser, in which we had to follow clues that led to the name of a location in Jerusalem. Everyone participated enthusiastically, and the grand prize for the winners was half a bar of chocolate, the generous contribution of the food committee.

About two weeks after the doctors' visit, general medical checkups began again. At the end of May, the Syrians took the amputees to the hospital to measure them for prostheses.

"Get ready, we're about to win the 'going home' lottery," I said confidently to my companions, who had also begun to think this might be the real reason behind the Syrians' intense interest in our health.

Each morning, the wounded would leave for the hospital, and in the evening they returned in lifted spirits. They told us about the doctors and the nurses. After several days of going back and forth to the hospital, they returned walking proudly on their new prostheses. We honored them by standing in two lines, and as they paraded down the middle, we cheered and clapped in delight.

The next day, the Syrians gathered all the wounded and took them away again. We awaited their return that evening, but in vain. Worry gnawed at us. Where had they disappeared to? "They're still in the hospital," the guard explained to us. After another day passed without a word from them, we decided to bribe the guard with an electric shaver. "They've returned to Israel," he grudgingly revealed.

On Monday, June 3, the jailer entered and called out six names, among them my own. Quickly we put on the new Syrian uniforms we had received in honor of the occasion and parted from our friends with emotion. We were certain we were on our way home.

They covered our eyes with sealed cloth blindfolds, then led us down the stairs and outside the building. This was the first time I had left the room without the black sack on my head, a notable experience. They put us inside a car, where total darkness surrounded us. No one said a word. The heat inside the car was insufferable, and I could barely breathe. I knew my friends were sitting on either side of me, but were we alone? Very slowly I lifted the blindfold from one eye. We were inside a closed police car used for transporting prisoners. The windows were sealed with boards. On the line of seats in front of me sat six people with black sacks on their heads. I had never seen this sight from an observer's point of view, and a chill passed through me at the memory of my own experiences. Two military policemen sat behind a screen door that served as a divider. I thought they would tell me to cover my eyes again, but they just looked at me in silence. Hesitantly, I lifted the black sack from the head of one of the soldiers sitting across from me, revealing a frightened face.

"Who are you?" I asked.

"Baruch Hayat," the soldier answered me.

"Are you a tanker?"

"No, I'm a medic." I understood that this was a group of enlisted men. I threw a glance at the two guards. They were sitting and chatting, and they didn't seem to mind if we talked as well.

"Guys, you can take off the blindfolds and the sacks," I said quietly, and they did so.

We began to talk and exchange information, but then the Syrians shouted at us to put the blindfolds back on. When we got out of the car, they removed the blindfolds and the sacks, and arranged us in pairs of officers and enlisted men. Then they led us inside a school. A great crowd filled the yard, and a chain of military police wearing red berets made sure no one approached us. They ordered us to hold hands, and we walked in line into a small classroom with four rows of benches. I sat in the far right row across from the door. Next to me sat Avi Zucker, an intelligence soldier who spoke Arabic and had been caught on the Hermon. A large man with black hair and impressive features entered the room along with a few escorts. He stood next to the blackboard and spoke in English. "Hello, I'm writing about the Palestinian problem, and I would like to hear your opinions on the subject."

"Guys, don't talk to him until he introduces himself!" I shouted in Hebrew. My interruption shocked him a bit. The others in the room also widened their eyes in surprise, but the elegant man continued to speak calmly. "My name is Dr. Rifa'i," he said.

"What, you know Hebrew?" I asked in a slightly antagonizing tone, but he chose to ignore my question. He signaled for one of his escorts to go over to me and continued speaking. A young man with a permanent smile hurried to me, bent down a bit and said, "You're an officer, right?" I realized he knew more about me that I had thought.

"Yes," I answered.

"If so, it's important for us to know your opinion on the Palestinian problem."

I was really not concerned with the Palestinian problem at that time, and I tried to put him off.

"Do you have a cigarette?" I asked him in Hebrew, miming a smoking movement with my hand. He took out a pack of cigarettes and gave me one.

"You know, I have a friend in the cell who smokes Parliament cigarettes. He really likes Parliaments. Give me one for him, too." Without a protest, he gave me two more cigarettes, hoping I would start talking.

"I'm very hungry, and when I'm hungry I can't talk about the Palestinian problem," I said, clutching my stomach in case he didn't understand me.

He turned around and whispered something to one of the soldiers. Then he turned back toward me, blocking me so that I would not disturb Dr. Rifa'i.

I looked at him in amusement, and then the door opened and they placed a colorful cream cake on the table before me. My mouth began to water. It was the prettiest, most colorful, and most tempting thing I had seen in eight months. I brought the tray close to my mouth and devoured the cake like a starving animal. Everyone there stared in amazement, but I did not care. Reveling in the sweet icing, I finished the entire cake and licked my lips and fingers.

I took a deep breath as if about to burst, and then another soldier came in carrying a second cake. I gestured for him to send it on back to me, and slapped my stomach with pleasure.

"Now talk!" the man with the permanent smile ordered victoriously.

"I'm thirsty. I want some beer." I decided to indulge myself.

"We don't drink beer. We only drink Bebsi," he said, the smile never leaving his face.

I didn't know what Bebsi was, but I thought that if they drank it, then it couldn't be poison.

"Okay, bring me some of that," I compromised.

The smiling man turned around, but then one of our soldiers stopped him and asked for a drink as well. When I saw that my order was delayed, I got up from my seat and shouted, "Your buddy Dr. Rifa'i said he would bring me Bebsi, but see how he's taking his time and not bringing it to me." The people in the room chuckled, and Dr. Rifa'i lost his patience and began to roar. Two jailers standing near the door jumped at me. They grabbed me by the arms and took me out of the room. Almost immediately, regret began to gnaw at my insides. Why had I caused all that commotion? Why couldn't I have told the Syrians what they wanted to hear about the Palestinians? Who knew what they would do to me now?

Then "Abu Pajama," who had been my first interrogator, came up to me and ordered the guards to release me. "Wow, great – Amenon," he said, mispronouncing my name. "It's good you came," he said cheerfully, and his enthusiasm reassured me. I walked down the stairs at his side, with no guard, my hands free and my eyes uncovered. He led me into a large hall in the basement. Projector lights blinded me, and television cameramen and reporters raced to and fro. I've fallen out of the fat and into the fire, I thought. I wouldn't talk in the classroom, so now I'll have to talk in front of the whole world. They sat me on a chair, put makeup on me and instructed me to sit beside a table in the center of the stage. I was very excited. No one had ever organized a press conference in my honor. Meanwhile, another entourage of reporters came in, among them a young woman with long hair flowing past her shoulders. She wore a tight blouse that emphasized her figure and tight stretch pants with straps under her feet. She sat down next to me and addressed me in Hebrew.

"Shalom, what is your name?"

"Amnon," I answered, breathing in the expensive perfume wafting from her.

"Where were you born and what is your marital status?"

"I was born in Cyprus. I'm married and I have two children, one a newborn baby," I answered with the pride of a new father.

She explained to me that she wanted to interview me for a program in Hebrew on Syrian television. I could not understand what the Syrians wanted with Hebrew, but I nodded my head reluctantly.

The director came and took measurements with a light meter. Then he said something in Arabic to the reporter, and the ancient cameras began to clatter.

"Good evening to our viewers at home," the young woman began. "We have here with us an Israeli prisoner-of-war, an officer, whom I will now interview. Good evening to you. What is your name?" she asked me.

"What do you think you're doing, making fun of me?" I asked her in front of the cameras. "I told you my name just two minutes ago! You've forgotten already?!"

"Cut!" screeched the director, and the astounded woman tried to explain to me that before was only a rehearsal, but now they were filming. Again she spoke to the cameras and I stopped her for a second time, until Abu Pajama got angry at my contemptuous behavior and signaled for two soldiers to take me upstairs.

They took me into a small room, where I confronted a tall, fat Syrian in civilian clothes and a soldier armed with a Kalashnikov. I shook with fear, and my bladder almost burst. "Toilet, toilet," I begged the fat one, but he waved a threatening hand and shut me up.

I sat quietly and thought about my antics that day and about the punishment awaiting me. Then I had a brilliant idea. I began to tell him a story in Hebrew. "You know, when the jailer would bring me food, he would always say to me, '*hud lach ya ars.*'" The Syrian nodded his head, appalled at this curse I had just uttered. I continued, "I always thought that *hud lach ya ars* meant 'bon appetit' in Arabic." He looked at me, entertained, and burst out laughing. "When the Red Cross came to visit us, they brought us chocolate," I said, trying to choke back my own laughter. "I went up to the Syrian colonel who accompanied them, offered him the chocolate and said, '*hud lach ya ars.*'" The fat guy clutched his stomach, which was shaking with laughter, and translated my story to the soldier. Still laughing, the three of us went off to the bathroom.

At the end of that evening we returned to the prison, and I gave Meir the two Parliaments I had received from Dr. Rifa'i's aide. I felt proud that I had managed to return safe and sound without having contributed to the Syrian propaganda machine.

The next evening, Tuesday, a guard came in and ordered us to get dressed and prepare to go out. He repeatedly emphasized that we should all eat and drink our fill, because there would be no food later.

Once again they covered our eyes with the black blindfolds, and took us in covered, suffocating trucks to the same school we had visited the previous day. They brought us to the large hall with the television cameras and projector lights and sat us in rows, officers in front and enlisted men in back. Policemen surrounded us. The door opened, and in walked Dr. Rifa'i with the "Yemenite" translator from the first interrogations.

Dr. Rifa'i talked about the Palestinian problem and the evil deeds we had done to them in 1948. The "Yemenite" translated for him. When he finished, he asked, "Are there any questions?" One of the officers spun around and shouted, "Don't ask anything, guys!" But many people raised their hands and asked questions anyway. Dr. Rifa'i's answers were repetitive and focused on the injustices the Israelis had carried out against the Palestinians.

Because it was a Tuesday, our bridge and movie day, I decided to put an end to this waste of time. I raised my hand and received permission to speak. "Dr. Rifa'i, I would like to conclude this wonderful evening. In Israel I have a publishing house, and I would like to publish your book." The Israelis burst out laughing. After the "Yemenite" translated what I had said, Rifa'i shouted in Arabic, "Just one minute ago your friends asked why Arabs and Jews don't get along, and here you are ruining things. We want to sit and talk, and you're not willing!"

"This is how you invite us for a chat? You haven't offered us even a drop of water!" I answered, inciting a wave of laughter even louder than the previous one. The doctor went wild with fury. He waved a hand to the policemen, who shouted at us to get up. They took us back to the prison, where confusion reigned. They put some of the enlisted men into our room and some of the officers into the cells of the enlisted men. The guards had to work for hours to calm things down and restore order. As punishment, my fellow officers reprimanded me and suspended me from the bridge tournament. There was nothing left for me to do but sit and ponder the events of the last two days.

On Wednesday, a jailer came in and shouted, "*Wanu* Amnon Sharon?" My teeth chattered in fear – I was about to get what I deserved for my insolent behavior. I asked Amos to speak to him in Arabic and find out what they wanted from me. Amos translated that I should get ready to leave the cell. "Where are you taking me?" I asked. The jailer answered, "Put on the uniform. You're going out for a television interview." I got dressed quickly so as not to anger him. Before leaving, I said to the pilots in all seriousness, "Guys, remember that I'm leaving here in good health. If by chance they get rid of me, send my greetings to everyone back home. I love you all."

We went to the office of "Abu Pajama." I sat down across from him, and he smiled and offered me a cigarette. "Amnon, you're going to be interviewed for French television. You'd better remember only the good times you had in Damascus," he said. Then they took me to a room and sat me in front of a television camera. While the staff got organized, I managed to exchange a few words with the cameraman, using the Arabic I had learned in Amos's class.

"Where are our friends, the…," I moved my hand over my leg to indicate "amputees."

"Israel, Israel," he said.

"And when is our turn?" I was pleased at the opportunity to obtain some secret information.

"*Yom al jum'a.*" I understood that on Friday, we would be going home.

At the end of the interview, they took me back to the cell. I called everyone together and told them the news.

The committees convened for discussion. We decided that despite the busy schedule, we would hold our farewell party that very evening, so that on Thursday we could go to sleep early and arrive home refreshed. The vote was unanimous, and we got to work. The food committee enlisted reinforcements and began to prepare the festive meal. Several of us gathered in a corner to rehearse the entertainment. The decorations committee made toilet paper chains and hung them around the room. In the evening, we put on our best clothes, and we ate, danced, and sang well into the night.

Despite our great excitement, we fell on our beds, exhausted but content, and fell asleep at once.

FREEDOM

On Thursday at dawn, one day earlier than we had thought, the prison guards burst into the room. "Quick, put on the Syrian uniforms and get ready to go out. Take nothing with you!" they shouted. They were more excited than we were. Everything happened too quickly – we could not understand what was going on. We had no time to get emotional, to say good-bye to the guards, or even to throw a last glance at the room that had become our home over the last few months.

I wore a blue T-shirt and the black shorts I had received from Israel. Just in case they searched us, I rolled up my letters from home inside the hem of my shorts. On top of the shorts I wore the Syrian uniform and the cloth shoes. I put a box of Syrian cigarettes into my pocket as a souvenir. In my hand I held the string of olive pits with the towel-thread pompom that I had made in the macramé class.

When we were ready, they took us outside, eyes uncovered. We rode in army buses in the direction of the Damascus airport, where the families of the Syrian prisoners awaited the return of their loved ones.

We were very excited. Finally, the day had arrived, the day we had looked forward to for many long months and for which we had suffered unbearable torments. Our departure from prison was as hasty as the Exodus from Egypt. It even took place two days before the date I had foreseen in my dream.

At a signal, they put us onto a Red Cross plane. "Abu Pajama" stood in the doorway and shook our hands in farewell, and we took our seats. On the plane we discovered other prisoners who had not been with us. One of these was Benny Kariati. Another was Ze'ev

Nesher, the man whom the pilots had mistaken me for when I had first entered the shared room. I sat next to Meir, my flight instructor. He kept nagging me throughout the entire flight, saying the first thing I should do after we landed was to ask the commander of the air force for a ride in a Phantom.

In the afternoon, the plane landed at the military airfield at Ben Gurion airport. Crowds awaited us, waving their hands and cheering.

Exactly one week previously, we had gone to the airport to greet the wounded prisoners. Their physical state was reasonably good. They were wearing prostheses and looked strong and optimistic. They also assured us that Amnon was in good health. Our joy was so intense that it was difficult for us to return home.

And then, on June 6, 1974, I found myself waiting at the airport along with Amnon's parents and a huge crowd. My parents had to stay at home with Dror and with Raviv, who had come down with the mumps that very week. We sat next to Prime Minister Golda Meir. She remembered Amnon's parents from their stay in the DP camp on Cyprus, where she had worked as an aliyah activist, and they had a nostalgic chat about those days.

The wait was nerve-racking and seemed to go on forever. I longed to see what he looked like and to hug him again. As the moment approached, the tension heightened.

"Here they come!" The crowd cheered and stood on its feet. The ceremony organizers roared into the microphones, exhorting the crowd to maintain order and quiet, and to allow Golda Meir to speak, but no one listened.

The first prisoner burst out of the airplane door, and my heart pounded. He looks pretty good, I said to myself, feeling a sense of relief. After him the prisoners came out one by one. They were very thin, but clean and wearing sportswear. They seemed happy, like youths who had just returned from an exhausting school trip.

The enlisted men were the first to push their way out, and Meir and I decided to wait for the crowd to subside a bit. I searched the window for Bella and my family. Behind me stood Meir, who kept badgering me to speak with the air force commander. "Amnon," he said, punching me on the shoulder, but I was in no hurry to reply. "Amnon, now!" he shook me stubbornly. I pulled my eyes away from the window and turned to Meir. Before me stood no less than General Benny Peled, commander of the air force. Moti Hod, director-general of the ports authority, was next to him. "Ask him now! Ask the commander if you can fly in a Phantom," Meir continued, muttering through his teeth as he smiled at the commander and the director.

In the armored corps, we maintain a certain distance between the various ranks. How could I possibly approach a general? Besides, I was not properly dressed – exercise pants, a T-shirt and cloth shoes. But Meir was more determined than me. He gave me a gentle push. Like a child running to greet his parents, I spread my hands out to my sides and called, "Benny!" Benny also stretched out his arms, hugged me and patted my head. "How are you?" he asked, and I answered, "I'm okay. I want to fly in a Phantom."

"Don't worry, you'll get to fly plenty," he promised, slapping me on the shoulder.

"But I'm a tanker," I said, so as to avoid disappointment should my request go unfulfilled. But he smiled at me again and said, "Don't worry, you'll fly."

I thanked him politely and smiled at Meir in relief. I had given it my best shot.

It was early afternoon, and the light of the June sun was blinding. I had spent the last eight months in dark cells, and when they took me outside, they covered my eyes with a black sack, and I worried that my family would think I was blind. I squinted as hard as I

could and prepared to get off the plane. Avikam Liff, who had been
wounded in prison and had gone home a week before us, came up
to meet us. He looked like a guardian angel, dressed handsomely
and carrying a bouquet of flowers in his hand. Over his eyes he
wore stylish Ray-Ban sunglasses, signature wear for Israeli pilots
in those days. I was overjoyed to see him. Embarrassed, I asked
him to lend me his sunglasses until I got off the plane, and he did
so with pleasure. I stood on the airplane ramp, thin as a rail. With
my sporty outfit and the Ray-Ban sunglasses adorning my face, I
waved to my family like a movie actor.

> *"Look how handsome he looks, like a movie actor. He even
> looks good thin." My mother-in-law pointed to him in joy
> and her eyes sparkled. I smiled, agreeing with every word.*

Bella was the first to race at me from the crowd, and my parents hurried behind her. I searched the crowd for my mother- and
father-in-law as well, thinking they would be waiting for me with
Raviv and Dror, but they had stayed home to look after the kids.
My greatest wish at that moment was to go home, take a refresh-
ing shower, and hug the kids. Then I would sit peacefully with my
family around the table and eat a rich meal, since in our haste we
had not eaten breakfast.

But dreams are one thing, reality another. We stood hugging
each other until two women officers from the air force gently de-
tached me from my family. They each held one of my hands and
led me into the base, while my family followed behind. We entered
a shaded area bordered by camouflage screens, where tables were
loaded with cakes, drinks, and fruit. I tried to stop near one of the
tables, but the officers pulled me into a closed building.

They opened the door, and a current of air-conditioning hit
my face. A film crew documented our entrance with a large film
camera set up on a cart. The entire air force elite stood at the side
of the hall, and in front of me were tables set with white cloths and
plates like in a fancy restaurant. Someone indicated I should ap-

proach the group of senior personnel. I couldn't understand how not one person from the armored corps had come to greet me. I shook the officers' hands. When I reached the last in line, the head of the personnel squadron, he asked me, "Who are you?"

"I'm Amnon Sharon," I answered.

"You're not one of us," he declared. Then he turned to his companions. "Guys, he's not one of us." I felt a stab in my heart. The insult stung no less than the cigarette burns, the marks of which had begun to fade just shortly before my release.

As an aside, he instructed me to go with my family to the corner where the government representatives waited, including Golda Meir.

"Where did you bail out?" asked Yitzchak Rabin, who was then Minister of Labor and later replaced Golda Meir as prime minister. I knew that abandoning an airplane was called "bailing out," and from my friends' stories I knew that most of them had bailed out on the Tapline Road.

"On the Tapline Road," I answered – I really had abandoned my tank there. "I would like to go eat," I admitted to him wishfully. More than anything else, my attention was focused on my stomach, which had begun to rumble, and I hoped the minister would release me from his interrogation.

"Just a minute," he insisted. "Were you alone or with a crew?"

"With a crew."

"And did the second crew member also come back with you?"

I sensed I was getting into trouble, and I said, "Listen, the gunner was killed in my arms. The loader – I saw him jump. I pulled the driver from the tank. He was burning, but I think he was okay." (I didn't know then that he had been killed.) Rabin began to mutter, confused.

"I'm from the tanks," I admitted.

"I understood that, I just don't understand what you're doing here."

I smiled at him in understanding. I had always known that pilots were a special race. Afterwards I learned there had been a separate reception for the "greens." Apparently, because of the Ray-Bans usually worn by Israeli pilots, the women escort soldiers had simply assumed I was one of them, and had led me to the air force reception tent.

A few minutes after admitting I wasn't a pilot, I parted from Rabin, and they led me behind the distinguished guests and out of the hall to a shelter made of camouflage netting. I ate with gusto from the plates loaded with seasonal fruit. It was so pleasant for me to sit with my family and fill the void of the past months. We began a light conversation. I wanted to know how the kids were and why Raviv had not come. I asked Bella how she had felt on her own during the pregnancy and how the birth had gone. I inquired about my business and whether they had sold the car as I had requested, and asked many other questions about what they had done during my absence.

I stood hugging Bella, and while my mouth was still full of a handful of juicy, cold grapes, a charming female soldier took me away from my wife and led me to the showers along with the other prisoners. "Here they will disinfect you and give out uniforms," she said, and no one considered protesting. After we were fitted out, I asked to speak with the head of military intelligence, General Shlomo Gazit, about our suspicion that Amos had given away a great deal of information during interrogations. He said they were aware of the issue and were taking care of it in their own way.

In the taxi home, Bella told me about her experiences since the day I had left home. She spoke of how hard it had been to take care of Raviv alone while pregnant with another child, who as far as she knew might be born orphaned of his father. As she talked, I noticed how she weighed each word. I examined the faces of my family, and saw they were being careful not to offend me. They were thinking carefully about what to say and how to avoid distressing me. It was a very strange situation: on the one hand they longed to be close to me, but on the other, they were afraid to hurt me with their curiosity and intense desire for intimacy.

The neighborhood had prepared a moving reception. Crowds

waited with signs, and schoolchildren from the Ayalon School where Bella taught stood in rows and held flags. The house was full of bouquets. Raviv, who had come down with the mumps the day before, lay sleeping on the couch in the living room. When I smothered him with hugs and kisses, he woke up somewhat frightened. He had a hard time recognizing me, and the crowd around us also confused him. I gave him the gifts I had saved from the packages of Israeli candy we had received in prison. Then he recovered himself and sat close to me. "Finally my dad's come home like all the other dads," he said, bringing tears of joy to my eyes. Then I rushed to the other room to meet Dror, my new son. He was sleeping in his crib, calm and peaceful, ignoring the tumult that filled the apartment. For a moment I even wondered if he was all right.

The guests continued to flow into the house, bringing all kinds of good things with them. I excused myself to my room to take off the uniform and put on my own clothes, but they were huge on me. I had gone to war weighing 203 pounds (ninety-two kilos), and now I weighed a mere 104 pounds (forty-seven kilos). All the belts I owned were too wide for my narrow hips, and I tied my pants with a piece of string so they wouldn't fall down.

During the weekend, dozens of visitors came to our house – family, friends, and acquaintances. We were showered with bouquets, as well as baked goods, fruit and other foods. Our happiness knew no bounds. Slowly my brain began to register the stories about everything that had happened during the eight months of my absence. My friends gradually revealed the names of comrades who had been killed in the war. They told me that Uzi, the battalion commander, had been seriously injured. He had been blinded in both eyes and had lost a hand. With a flash of pain, I recalled that after I had abandoned my tank and run across the field among the other burning tanks, I had seen a hand lying on the ground.

The story of Uzi shook me. I wanted to see him desperately, give him a hug, and thank him personally for his warm treatment of my family. Because of him, they sustained the hope of finding me alive. I continued to ask about my friends and about the tank

crew, particularly Moshe Karasenti, my driver. Moshe was from
Migdal, a *moshav* near Tiberias. We had served together since our
compulsory service, and continued together in the reserves. After
I had pulled him out of the burning tank, we rolled together on
the ground and smothered the flames. Then I told him to run toward Nafah while I continued rounding up my wounded soldiers.
Throughout my stay in prison, I had wondered what had happened
to him, but I was sure he had been saved.

"The Syrians caught him and killed him," said one of my friends
who came to visit. "But that's not all," he continued sadly. One of
the guys discovered his body, and out of good will this guy decided to take Moshe's identification, his watch and his personal
belongings and give them to his family. Moshe's house was always
open to soldiers on their way to military operations in the Golan
Heights. We used to stop at his place in Migdal, and his mother
would bake us cakes and serve us nuts and drinks. This friend felt
a personal obligation to return Moshe's belongings himself. Then
the war broke out, and the entire brigade, including the soldier
who took Karasenti's things, went down to Egypt to Kilometer
101. Meanwhile, Karasenti was buried in Migdal and his parents
sat *shiva* for him.

A month later, during a slight pause in the fighting, this friend
remembered Karasenti's belongings, and decided to give them to
the adjutant in Sinai to send them to the family. The adjutant followed regulations and sent them to the Tiberias city officer. Accompanied by a doctor and a psychologist, the city officer's staff
went to inform Karasenti's family that he had been killed and that
they had his documents. "We know, we've already buried him and
sat *shiva*," the parents said. "That can't be, here is his identification
and his belongings, sent from the south," the city officer insisted,
showing them the identify card, the watch and a bracelet. Everyone
was confused. The parents were convinced that their son had fought
in the north and was killed there, while the city officer insisted he
had received the items from the south. Finally, they opened the
grave to check, but some uncertainty still remained. 'Maybe he's in

prison with Amnon,' the parents hoped. 'They were always together.'
Even when Kissinger brought the list of prisoners and Karasenti's
name was not on it, the father still believed his son had given the
Syrians a made-up name. When we came home, he waited until
the last of the prisoners came out of the airplane. When he saw
that his son was not among them, he returned to Migdal, went to
the cemetery and shot himself on his son's grave.

A troubled silence filled the room. The story of Karasenti
brought me back to the horror, and with great sorrow I told my
friends I needed to rest.

RECOVERY CLINIC IN
ZICHRON YA'AKOV

On Sunday morning, a taxi came to my house. It drove me and several other released prisoners to a recovery clinic in Zichron Ya'akov that had been transformed into an army base.

At the clinic, reporters and television crews awaited us. Tables of refreshments stood outside, and the atmosphere was pleasant, like in a convalescent home. Shortly after our arrival the first of the pilots began to arrive, and to my great surprise, they were all driving fancy Fiat 132s. An air force liaison officer received them and accompanied them to their rooms. Despite the great respect I had gained for the pilots and the air force, I was annoyed that we "greens" who had returned from captivity were considered unworthy of the special conditions the "blues" enjoyed. After lunch, I went to the commander of the facility and asked for a car like my friends had received, but unfortunately, my request was refused.

In the evening, Musa Peled, armored corps commander, arrived along with Ehud Gross, his office manager. They gathered all the armored corps men together for a talk, about seven of us. At first everything went smoothly. Musa asked about our health. He wanted to know if we had any special problems, and inquired how he could help. Then the conversation took a different turn, and he asked, "How is it that you went out to war without equipment, without ammunition, and without adjusting your sights?" At first I did not fully understand his meaning, and I was confused by his attack. But his words hurt like knives opening my wounds. My comrades and I had held back the enemy with dilapidated tanks and without ammunition because we understood that the situation was desperate and we had no choice. "We were cannon fodder, and where were you? Weren't you aware of the situation?!" I shouted back at him. I limped out of the room, fuming but above all frustrated and wounded by the heavy accusations.

We stayed in the Zichron facility for a few days, during which we were debriefed on field security. In captivity, I had memorized all the information I had given to the Syrians so that I could report it in Israel. During the debriefings, I had ample chance to tell everything I knew and release all the tension.

After a struggle, I received a small car, and at the end of each day I chose to go home and be with my family. In the mornings I returned to Zichron for more activities: debriefings, preliminary psychological treatment, and entertainment programs. I also underwent medical examinations, in which I was found both physically injured and emotionally traumatized.

One evening I had the pleasure of meeting Simcha Holzberg, "father of the wounded." I stood outside with a group of friends as a cluster of people approached us. Someone pointed to me and declared, "Hey, there's Amnon Sharon." A religious man wearing a gray suit and a brimmed hat strode in the center of the group. He approached me and offered his hand. "I'm so pleased to meet you," he said, shaking mine warmly. "I represented you at Dror's *brit milah*. I knew you were over there, and the rest you probably know." Indeed, I knew everything, as the first things Bella had told me about were the deeds of this wonderful man. He had offered to help when Dror was born and continued to take an interest in them and in me until our meeting in Zichron. Simcha Holzberg embraced me and recounted how he had worried for me and prayed for my safe return. I was very pleased at the opportunity to meet this marvelous "*mitzvah* man" whose reputation preceded him.

As part of the treatments, they assigned me a psychologist, Dr. Morris Kleinhaus. I had never seen a psychologist before except in the movies, where they were always serious, elderly men who spoke calmly and wore round eyeglasses. Dr. Kleinhaus did wear eyeglasses, but he did not insist that I lie on a couch and talk, like in the movies. Instead, he accompanied me everywhere I went, living my daily routine along with me. Together we played ping-pong and walked along the paths of the facility. "Talk," he would say in the midst of an activity. "Tell me what you feel. Don't keep anything inside. Get it all out." This was not an easy task. I am a reserved person by nature, and I was not used to talking about myself. "Imagine you're on a tank and you have to jump off," he insisting, taking me back to those difficult moments.

"I can barely walk on my wounded feet, and you want me to jump from a tank?" I couldn't understand what he wanted from me.

"You should know, Amnon, that people with injuries worse than yours have gotten back inside tanks and served as senior commanders in the armored corps." He stood his ground, and to this day I thank him for it, because I got the message. With that, the psychological treatment ended.

As part of the recuperation program, we went on trips. One of these was to the Knesset to hear a discussion about the Syrians' treatment of Israeli prisoners of war. We sat in the guests' balcony, and then the Knesset members invited us to eat lunch with them. Next to me sat MK Shmuel Tamir. We exchanged a few words, and as he bit into his chicken breast he said, "For my part, I wouldn't have brought you back. The state paid a very high price for you. Nothing bad would have happened if you had stayed there a while longer. In the end the Syrians would have broken down and sent you home." I put my forkful of meat down onto my plate, and without a word got up and left the room. The only thing I wanted at that moment was to be alone. I went outside and sat on the grass, and thought about the price that we, the prisoners, had paid on behalf of the state. Scars on our bodies and souls, missing limbs, and trauma would haunt us for the rest of our lives.

One day, Brigade Commander Ran Sarig came to visit me.

"In the Yom Kippur War, the 179th Brigade, the most senior of the reserve brigades in the IDF, was the first and fastest brigade to mobilize its reservists. We began holding actions against the

Syrians within twelve hours of being called up," he reported, with obvious pride. I wanted to hear about the brigade's experiences from the moment Uzi and I had left Camp Fillon. He told me how the brigade had proceeded after that point. Tanks arrived from other war reserves storage units, and some followed us over the Bnot Ya'akov Bridge up to the Golan, while the remainder of the brigade took the Arik Bridge.

"Aerial photographs from the morning of Sunday, October 7, 1973, show that your company halted ninety-four Syrian tanks," he said. I was relieved that finally, here was someone who understood what he was talking about, who was familiar with events the way they had occurred, and who appreciated that we had stood firm despite the impossible conditions.

Ran also told me that after the holding actions, the brigade pierced the Syrian alignments, conquered the Syrian enclave, and fought Jordanian and Iraqi forces, coming to within thirty-five kilometers (twenty-two miles) of Damascus. Then the brigade went down to Sinai, where they reached the 101st kilometer (sixty-third mile) from Cairo, a marker that went down in history.

When Ran finished his story, he asked me if I wanted to join him for a short trip. We got into his jeep and drove to the Tapline Road, to the place where my company had been hit. My heart began to pound. The stony hill where I had lain wounded until the Syrians caught me stood silent. Here and there on the large stones I could see black stains, vestiges of the fire, but there was no trace of all the blood that had been spilled there. I tried to look for the documents I had buried in the dirt, but couldn't find the right place.

Many dear friends and army personnel came to visit us in Zichron Ya'akov. One of the most fascinating and moving of these meetings was with battalion commander Uzi Mor. While I was at home, friends had updated me more or less regarding his condition. When he arrived, he walked toward me with confidence, so that it was hard to tell he was blind in both eyes. He came closer to me until he sensed my presence, stretched out his only hand, and clasped me to his chest. My throat was choked with tears, and I did not know how to react. But Uzi took the initiative and began to recount everything that had happened to him from the moment he was wounded. He told me about his rescue, his arrival at Rambam Hospital in Haifa with his hand hanging off his arm, and the amputation in the hospital. Then I understood that the hand I had seen in the field was not his. He also told me about Baruch, the deputy battalion commander with whom I had been inducted into the brigade. Baruch was killed along with Ijo Reinenbach, B Company commander. I felt intense pain. These soldiers were like my brothers. We had served together during our compulsory service and fought together in the Six-Day War. Together we were called up to the reserves, and together we went out to that terrible battle – but not all of us returned.

EPILOGUE

In a modest ceremony in Zichron Ya'akov, I was promoted to major. Following the recommendation of the psychologist and the medical staff, I signed on for one year of standing army service, until I could complete the operations I had to undergo.

While I awaited the operations, I worked at administrative and office jobs, which did not suit my character. So I called Musa Peled, armored corps commander, and asked him to put me back with the tanks.

A few days later, I was called to appear at the armored corps headquarters at Castina. I entered Peled's office and saluted him, and he returned the salute and got up to hug me. I sat across from him, excited, and then he informed me, "You're about to be appointed to a special, top secret position." He looked around to make sure no one was listening, leaned toward me, and continued, "You are going to carry out operational tests on the new Israeli tank, the Merkavah!" I smiled and told him that I had first heard the name "Merkavah" from the Syrians, and I was pleased to fulfill my dream. Beginning in July 1974, I performed all the tests on the Merkavah tank, and also wrote the doctrinal documentation. I had to undergo the first operation during the trials, but after it I returned to my position.

At the recommendation of Avigdor Kahalani, the commander of Tze'elim camp, I applied to the disability committee, and they determined that I had a certain level of disability. But for all the remaining years of my service I hid it from the soldiers. I ignored the pain and tried to fulfill all my duties despite my physical limitations.

Later the IDF asked me to take a command staff course, and I signed on for another five years of standing army service. During that time, I was appointed commander of a reserves battalion. I fought in Lebanon during Operation "Peace for Galilee," and then I took command of a compulsory service battalion in Sinai. After the pullout from Sinai I moved with the battalion to the Jericho region, and subsequently I returned to an administrative position as deputy head of doctrine for the armored corps.

By the time a company of Merkavah tanks first stood on a cement platform, I was a colonel. I stood in the tower at the Ze'elim tank range in the Negev, looking down with pride on twelve tanks. My eyes were damp with happiness. Here was my fleet of matchboxes, with cigarettes sticking out of each one for cannon barrels – my tank dream from Al-Mazeh prison had come true!

"I saw the tanks in this scene a few years ago," I said to the officer next to me.

"That can't be, this is the first time we have the Merkavah!" he said in surprise, and I smiled a secret smile.

As time went by, more issues came full circle for me. A few months after I returned to standing army service, the air force invited me to the Phantom squadron base at Tel Nof. On the appointed date, I presented myself in excitement, and none other than Lieutenant Colonel Snir greeted me. He had been the commander of the Phantom squadron back then. "I hope you haven't forgotten the promise General Benny Peled made to you," he said with a wide smile. "It's time we fulfilled it," he announced, and with no further ado, he led me to the Phantom of Avi Barber, my friend from prison. Together we flew across Israel's skies, and at the end of the flight they dunked me in a tub full of water, just like they do after a person performs his first solo flight.

I performed various command staff and training roles until my release from the army in 1988. After my release I fulfilled yet another dream. Together with my son Raviv, I established a factory for manufacturing beds and mattresses, not thin straw mattresses like we had in prison, but the ones I had seen in my dream.

On June 6, 2000, I left for the factory as usual at 4:30 A.M. The radio was playing a popular song, "Small Joys" by Micha Shitrit and Amir Banyon: "Praise, angels will praise you / And you won't lose your way in the brightness or in the dark / Praise, angels will praise you / Small joys will shine like the sparkle of the stars." This is an appropriate song for the twenty-sixth anniversary of my return from captivity, I thought. This will be a day for good news. Indeed, late that morning Raviv called me. "*Mazal tov*, you're a grandfather," he congratulated me. On that wonderful day my first grandson, Ro'i, was born. That same day my daughter Lihi also phoned. "Dad, you can congratulate me. I was promoted to lieutenant." Tuesday was my lucky day twice over.

There are some things that do not heal with time, but are merely blurred with the force of habit. The soles of my feet, which suffered so many beatings, constantly trouble me, but I am used to pain and I live with it. My fingers lost their feeling, which can cause embarrassment when I need to shake someone's hand. The advantage of the lack of feeling is that when someone needs to open a stubborn bottle top or free a rusty screw, I am able to perform the mission easily.

Because of the severe whippings and injuries, I do not like to be touched. Every touch feels like a beating.

"You have a very good memory, and this is your blessing as well as your curse," they told me at the end of the medical examinations at Levinstein Rehabilitation Hospital. I still suffer from post-traumatic stress syndrome, and remain awake for most of the day and night. I do not have nightmares, but the memory of my time in prison remains within me – the pain, the anxiety and the fears.

I am constantly tense. Any sudden noise startles me, every slam of a door makes me jump. The clapping of hands reminds me of the guards rushing me to the tortures in prison. Certain events and figures recall the torments of captivity.

I left prison injured in body, but newly forged in soul. My spirit is stronger than ever, because God is inside my heart. He carries me in His hands, and we walk together in the same footprints.

APPENDIX

MY PERSONAL PRAYER

I composed this personal prayer while in captivity.
It brought me comfort and filled me with faith and hope.
I continue to say this prayer every day of my life:

"Shema Yisrael – Hear O Israel, the Lord is God, the Lord is One.
Blessed are You, Lord our God, King of the universe, through whose
word everything came to be. Blessed are You, Lord our God, King
of the universe, through whose word everything is done. Lord God,
give me strength to continue, keep me healthy, protect me and my
family. Amen, amen, amen."

"שמע ישראל, ה' אלוקינו ה' אחד. ברוך אתה ה' אלוקינו מלך
העולם שהכול נהיה בדברו, ברוך אתה ה' אלוקינו מלך העולם
שהכול נעשה בדברו, ה' אלוקים, תן לי כוח להמשיך, תן לי בריאות,
שמור עליי ועל משפחתי, אמן, אמן, אמן."

IN MEMORY OF

At a meeting with the families of my comrades who fell in the war, I heard one mother ask painfully:

"How is it that no one has ever written about the part in the war played by the 179th Reserve Brigade? After all, they were the first to block the Syrian attack. How is it that their contribution to the war, which cut off their dreams, their youth, and their lives, has never been commemorated?"

Her words affirmed a desire that was engrained within me for many years – to document my personal story. I decided to realize it.

Thus I hereby dedicate this book to all those who fell in Israel's defense and whose stories are unknown, and especially to the survivors and the fallen of the 179th Reserve Brigade, who will always be my brothers.

May their memory be blessed forever

First Sergeant Moshe Karasenti
Son of Tikvah and Gavriel
Fell in the Hushniye area
On October 6, 1973
Aged 25 on his death

Sergeant Shlomo Tubi
Son of Malka and Chaim
Fell in the Tapline Road
On October 6, 1973
Aged 25 on his death

First Sergeant Ahron Ahroni
Son of Miriam and Avraham
Fell in the holding action combat
On October 6, 1973
Aged 24 on his death

Sergeant Moshe Avnaim
Son of Seniora and Shmaryahu
Fell in the holding action combat
On October 6, 1973
Aged 24 on his death

Sergeant Major Eliezer Lietner
Son of Sara and Joseph
Fell in the holding action combat
On October 7, 1973
Aged 25 on his death

BATTLE DIARY OF THE 179TH RESERVE BRIGADE – YOM KIPPUR WAR, OCTOBER 1973

OCTOBER 5

At 8:00 A.M., the brigade's regular army soldiers go on leave for the Yom Kippur holiday. Two hours later, brigade headquarters receives orders to put the regular army on alert. Soldiers return from leave throughout the day. The battalion commanders and principal staff are alerted.

OCTOBER 6, YOM KIPPUR

At 9:50 A.M., headquarters gives orders to call up the brigade. The call-up network is immediately activated. By 2:00 P.M., most of the commanders and staff members posted to the Golan have arrived. Uzi's battalion is designated to lead. His soldiers equip themselves and receive their tanks at the brigade base. Members of the two other battalions ride transports to another brigade base to receive tanks.

At 10:00 P.M., Uzi's first force leaves for the Nafah area to initiate contact with the enemy on the Tapline Road. About half an hour later, this first force enters into battle.

OCTOBER 7

At 1:15 A.M., the second half of the battalion starts out toward the Nafah region and enters into combat on the Tapline Road and the Sindiana–Hushniye road. By afternoon the Syrians wipe out this battalion in harsh combat, and it ceases to function.

5:00 A.M. In the early morning, the first force from Yisrael's battalion arrives at Arik Bridge and travels up the Yehudiya-Hushniye road. Half an hour later, it enters into combat near the abandoned Syrian village of Katzabiyeh. At the same time, the second half of Yisrael's battalion arrives and continues on Yehudiya road to join the fighting force near Katzabiyeh.

7:00 A.M. Yossi's battalion arrives at Arik Bridge and receives orders to go up to the Golan Heights on Skopyah Road in order to prevent the enemy from advancing from high on the Golan toward the south. By 2:00 P.M., this battalion single-handedly stops the Syrians on this road.

Later, one company in this battalion moves toward Katzabiyeh and joins the Israeli forces there. At 2:00 P.M., Yossi's battalion transfers to the command of another brigade and continues operating under its command until the end of the battles. By afternoon, most of the commanders of the 179th Brigade are wounded, including the deputy battalion commander, the battalion commander, and the brigade commander.

OCTOBER 8
Fighting starts again in the morning against the Syrian tank forces advancing from the direction of Hushniye. In the afternoon, the deputy brigade commander, Gideon Cimbel, is killed, and command of the brigade passes to the operations branch officer, Major Giora. Representing the brigade are Yisrael's battalion and the division patrol battalion, under the command of battalion commander Hanani.

OCTOBER 9
Amid harsh tank battles, the brigade pursues the offensive and advances toward Hushniye. In the evening, with the participation of Yossi's battalion, the brigade takes over Hushniye. Attacking from the north, it takes part in the all-division battle for the Hushniye alignment.

OCTOBER 10

Fighting continues in the direction of the Purple Line, pounding the enemy in the zone. Brigade forces reach Post 110 near Kuneitra, which the enemy had surrounded in the first hours of the fighting but which stood firm throughout the war.

The general staff cancels the order to break through the Purple Line into Syrian territory. The Syrians attack the brigade in its night encampment with heavy shelling.

The brigade commander returns from the hospital and retakes command, organizing the forces for the next stage of fighting. The brigade now includes Yisrael's battalion, the division patrol battalion, and a company from Yossi's battalion.

OCTOBER 11

The division receives orders for the breakthrough battle to the east. The brigade is appointed to go out first on the Kuneitra-Damascus road, with the goal of breaking through toward Han-Arnabeh junction. Zero-hour is designated as 1:30 P.M. Two battalions from the brigade push past Han-Arnabeh, with the patrol battalion spread out on the left and Yisrael's battalion, under the command of Major Giora, breaking into the road. Yisrael's battalion takes the junction. Of the thirty tanks leaving for the breakthrough battle, only five arrive intact at Han-Arnabeh junction. Two other brigades capitalize on the success of Yossi's battalion, passing through the junction to deepen the breakthrough. We spend the night of October 11–12 evacuating wounded from the battlefields and reorganizing.

OCTOBER 12

A tank company from "Nati Force" joins the brigade as reinforcements. It includes one battalion of tanks and one of APCs. It leaves Han-Arnabeh toward the Syrian pocket, in the direction of the Syrian village of Jaba, to form a blockade in case of an enemy counterattack from the south. Until 5:00 P.M., brigade forces are engaged in combat inside the pocket, in enemy territory. Then an order is received to return to the Kuneitra-Damascus line to confront a large Iraqi force ascending from Tel Shams. As the last light fades, brigade forces battle the rearguard of the Iraqi division.

OCTOBER 13

At first light, the brigade recommences battle in the pocket. Together with the rest of the division forces, brigade fighters close in on the Iraqi tank division, destroying one-third of it.

OCTOBER 15

The 179th Brigade fights a large Jordanian tank force and destroys twenty-eight of its tanks. In the afternoon, brigade forces face a Syrian-Iraqi counterattack.

OCTOBER 16

In the evening, the brigade receives orders to leave the lines for reorganization. At night, the forces move toward the reorganization camp in the Nafah region.

OCTOBER 20

On Saturday at 9:00 P.M., 179th Brigade begins to load tanks onto transports for the descent to Sinai.

OCTOBER 22

At 6:00 A.M., brigade forces cut across the Suez Canal and join Kalman division. After the crossing to the west, the brigade begins artillery shelling and air bombings. That same day, it takes over Kasparit airport. At dusk, brigade forces battle Egyptian armored forces on the Janifa-Cairo road, destroying eight tanks.

OCTOBER 23

In the afternoon, the brigade attacks an Egyptian brigade zone, where the Third Army command is located. The zone is conquered without losses to brigade forces. The 179th Brigade moves to cut off the Suez-Cairo road, and from there turns to join the division attack toward Al-Adabiyah. The brigade camps for the night in occupied Al-Adabiyah.

OCTOBER 24

At first light, the brigade conducts a search of the Al-Adabiyah area. In the afternoon, it begins to move back toward the Suez-Cairo road, toward Janifa junction, following orders to take the large Egyptian zone located there. The brigade is joined by a battalion from another brigade, which has already engaged the enemy near the junction. Using artillery and air, the brigade attacks the Egyptian zone from three directions.

The 179th Brigade conquers the zone as the last light begins to fade. The unit attached to the brigade in this battle turns west on the road to Cairo and stops at the 101st kilometer – a landmark that is to go down in history.

After conquering the large Egyptian zone near Janifa junction and taking over the 101st kilometer, the brigade concludes its role on the southern front. The forces organize to return north, except for one battalion, which remains on the west side of the Suez Canal for a few more weeks.

צבא הגנה לישראל
הקליטות הראשית
י' אדר תשל"ד
4 מרס 1974

אלפחת פינסו

משפחה יקרה,

בהמשך להודעתנו מיום ד' ה-27 בפברואר 1974,
על סיקירכם נמצא ברשימת הסבויים הישראליים בסוריה, הננו
שמחים להודיעכם, שנציג הצלב האדום הבין-לאומי ביקר את
סבויינו בסוריה ביום ד' ה-1 מרס 1974 ומצא את יקירכם
במצב גופני ומורלי טוב.

יקירכם ביקש מנציג הצלב האדום הבין-לאומי
למסור דרישת שלום למשפחתו וכמו כן את כרטיס השבוי, כפי
שנכתב על ידו.

נודיעכם מיד לכשיוובאו לידיעתנו פרטים נוספים

בברכה

השליש הראשי

Translation of the Hebrew letter ☞

OFFICIAL RED CROSS DOCUMENTS

Israel Defense Forces
Chief   Adjutancy
10   Adar   5734
March   4,   1974

To the Steinmetz Family:

Dear Family,

Following our letter of Wednesday, February 27, 1974, that your loved one is on the list of Israeli prisoners in Syria, we are pleased to inform you that the representative of the International Red Cross visited our prisoners in Syria on Friday, March 1, 1974, and found your family member in good physical and emotional condition.

Your family member asked the International Red Cross representative to send you his greetings as well as this prisoner card, written in his own handwriting.

We will inform you as soon as we receive any additional details.

Cordially yours,

The Chief Adjutant

127

צבא הגנה לישראל
המטה הכללי

_____

מרכז קשר למשפחות
נ צ ד ר י ם
תל. 2016
כ"ד ניסן תשל"ד
16 אפריל 74

ג י ל ו י

הרינו מאשרים בזה כי ל"פ הודעת ארגון הצלב האדום הבינלאומי נמצא החייל סרן אסנון סרון בשבי הסורי מאז מלחמת יום הכיפורים.

רב אלוף מנפל, סא"ל
ראש ומרכז

The official IDF letter declaring that as per the Red Cross notification, the author has been found as prisoner in Syria since the Yom Kippur war

CONTENTS OF THE FIRST PACKAGE SENT FROM ISRAEL TO THE POWS ON MARCH 17, 1974:

65 pairs of warm slippers
65 pairs of woolen socks
65 long undershirts
65 bars of soap
65 towels
65 pairs of underwear
65 toothbrushes
65 tubes of toothpaste
65 *haroset* plates for Passover
130 chocolate bars
3 packages of matzah
65 packages of instant soup
10 packages of tissues
5 tubes of mustard
6 bottles of black pepper
10 cans of peanuts in oil
10 cans of walnuts in oil
6 cartons of rice crispies
10 tubes of anchovy
12 cartons of pudding
2.2 pounds of salt
14 packages of biscuits
16 cans of stuffed fish
4 cans of preserved milk
20 cans of meat
2.2 pounds honey
6 jars of instant coffee
9 packages of tea bags
20 packages of soup nuts
65 moist handwipes
30 packages of sucking candy
65 packages of dried fruit

65 ball point pens
10 pads of paper (for writing)
3 strings of prayer-beads (for Bedouins)
3 flutes
3 harmonicas
3 springs for abdominal exercises
9 metal coils for hand exercises
12 packages of playing cards
3 kitchen utensils
3 chess sets
4 backgammon sets
4 domino sets
4 checkers sets
4 games of solitaire
6 painting kits
2 Monopoly games
1 box of mosaics
1 box of magic tricks

RELIGIOUS ARTICLES:
4 *tallitot* (prayer shawls)
62 yarmulkes
4 Bibles
1 Koran
4 prayer books
2 Passover Haggadahs

SENT SEPARATELY:
6 packages of matzah
Glasses
Medications

PHOTOS

This is how I was presented on the Syrian television news broadcast.

On October 23, 1973 this photo was published in an Italian newspaper
Domenica Del Corriere, in which we were described as Phantom pilots.

Later I found out that this photo taken by the Red
Cross representative was one of the few that depicted
the cell we were kept in while in captivity.

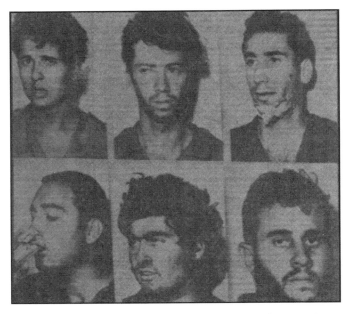

These photos were sent to Israel by the authorities in
Damascus after heavy pressure on behalf of Israel. In their
reports we were described as "commando fighters."

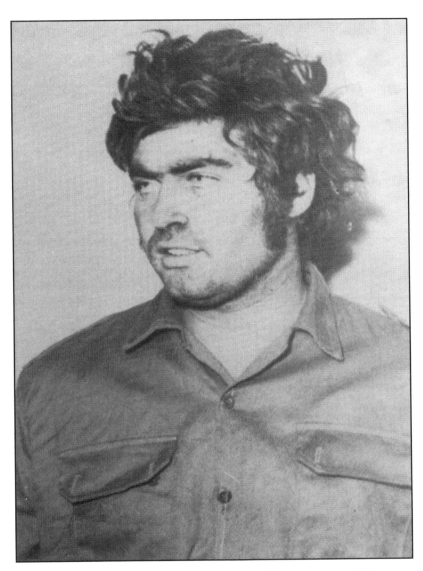

I had never understood the power of the camera until I
realized that this photo became my "life insurance."

The string of olive pits with the towel-thread pompon.

A photo from the attempted interview for French
television that "almost" succeeded.

On my return, I was excited to find out that this portrait, painted
by my father from an earlier photo of me, acted as a "substitute"
for me at the Shabbat and holiday tables while I was away.

NEWSPAPER ARTICLES FROM THE DAILY *MA'ARIV* AND *YEDIOT AHARONOT*

BORN IN PRISON AND BACK FROM PRISON
by Avraham Arnon
YEDIOT AHRONOT CORRESPONDENT

Amnon Sharon was born in the deportation camp in Cyprus. His parents, Holocaust survivors, were imprisoned there by the British for attempting to enter Palestine. Yesterday, Amnon returned to his home in Tel Aviv from another prison camp, the one in Damascus.

He was blessed with seeing his son Dror, born six weeks ago, for the first time. But because the baby was ill with mumps, the celebratory reception was held in Amnon's parents' house in Givatayim.

נולד בשבי
וחזר מהשבי

מאת
אברהם ארנון,
כתב "ידיעות אחרונות"

אמנון שרון נולד ב־
מחנה מעפילים בקפרי־
סין, שם נכלאו הוריו,
ניצולי השואה, אשר
נלכדו בידי הבריטים
בהעפילם ארצה. אתמול
חזר אמנון לביתו בתל־
אביב ממחנה אחר: מח־
נה השבויים בדמשק.

הוא זכה לראות, זו
הפעם הראשונה, את
בנו דרור, שנולד לפני
שישה שבועות. אבל, ל־
אחר שהתינוק חלה ב־
חזרת, נערכה קבלת הפ־
נים החגיגית דווקא
בבית הוריו של אמנון,
בגבעתיים.

137

קיבל שעון יקר במקום זה שנשדד ממנו ע"י הסורים

שעונו היקר, מתנת יחידת־שריון מהתקופה בצה"ל, ניתן כשי לסרן אמנון שרון. שחזר לא מכבר מהשבי הסורי בו נשדד ממנו שעונו.

את השעון, שהוגש על־ידי מפקד חטיבתו ואשר נתגם עליידי חברת "מרחיף", נחרת: "לאמנון, לדרור – מחבריך ליחידה".

אמנון שרון היה מפקד פלוגה. הוא פיקד על טנק שנפגע עוד בתחילת קרבות הבלימה ליד צ'יר'הנפטה. אך הצליח, עם עוד אחד מאנשי הצוות, לקפוץ מהטנק הפגוע. משהתברר לו שמוני אנשי הצוות הנותרים נשארו בבטן הטנק. החליט לנסות לחלצם על אף הסכנה שבדבר, הוא התקרב לטנק ואז אירעה התפוצצות, ועקבותיו נעלמו. לוהמם שהיו בשטחה אמרו כי לדעתם הוא נהרג, והתפוצץ יחד עם הטנק, אולם חבריו לנשק סירבו להאמין לסיפור והחליטו לחפש אחריו. כעבור ימים מספר, תוך המלחמה, התפנו לשם כך כמה מאנשי היחידה, חיפשו וחיפשו בטנק ולא מצאו בו שום שרידי־אדם. הם התחלו גם לסרוק את כל הסבבה, אך ללא תועיל. האדמה כאילו בלעה אותו, מאוחר יותר התברר לחבריו, כי מפקדם נלקח בשבי. אחד מקציני היחידה מצא עלון צבאי סורי בו פורסמו תמונותיהם של שבעה שבויים ישראלים, שאחד מהם היה אמנון.

עתה, לאחר שחרורו, סיפר אמנון את הקורות אותו באותו יום גורלי. לדבריו, הדף ההתפוצצות למרחק של כ־40 מטרים ונפל על גבו בלי יכולת לזוז. הוא שכב טענת מספר כך, בלי תנועה, עד שחושיו חזרו אליו וגם יכולת להתנועע. בינתיים נמשך, במקום, "יום העצמאות הסורי" כשאלפי חיילים, טנקים ונגמ"שים נוספים בשטח מבלי שאיש עוצר אותם... לאחר יותר מדמשה, בה היה בלי אוכל ושתיה, נעצר לידו טנק סורי שהתקלקל. אמנון חשב כי הרגישו בו, יצא ממחבואו התכונן להיכנע, אולם מפקד הטנק הסורי שחבנון בו, נבהל ונהדם את ידיו. אמנון, שלא ידע מה לעשות, ניסה להסביר לסורי המופתע כי למעשה הוא השבוי. כעבור מספר שניות הבין חלה את הרגעו, הוציא את אקדחו ובגד רועדת ציווה עליו ללכת אחריו. אמנון הועבר לבסיס סורי קרוב, שם לקחו ממנו את מסמכיו ואת שעונו. מבסיס זה הועבר לדמשק שבה שהה בבלא עד שחוריו. (פ)

Translation of the Hebrew Article ☞

RECEIVES LUXURY WATCH TO REPLACE
THE ONE STOLEN BY THE SYRIANS

The commander of one of the oldest armored units in the IDF presented a luxury watch to Amnon Sharon, who recently returned from imprisonment in Syria, where his own watch was stolen. The Marvine Company donated the watch, which was engraved with the words "To Amnon, to Dror – from your friends in the unit."

Amnon Sharon was a company commander. He had commanded a tank that was hit at the beginning of the holding action battles near the Tapline Road. Along with one of his crew members, Amnon jumped from the damaged tank. When he realized that the two remaining crew members were still inside the tank, he decided to try to rescue them, despite the inherent danger. When he approached the tank, it exploded, and he disappeared. Fighters in the area said that they thought he had been killed and that his body must have exploded along with the tank. But his company members refused to believe this and were determined to look for him. A few days later, while the war was still going on, several of the unit members made the time to search his tank. But they found no trace of a body inside. They began to comb the area, but without success. It was as if the ground had swallowed him. Later, Amnon's comrades learned that the Syrians had taken him prisoner. One of the unit officers found a Syrian military pamphlet with photographs of six Israeli prisoners. One of them was Amnon.

After his release, Amnon told the story of his experience on that fateful day. According to him, the explosions threw him about forty-five feet (fourteen meters) away, and he fell on his back unable to move. He lay that way for a few hours, motionless, until he regained his senses and his mobility. In the meantime, the Syrian parade of weaponry continued. Thousands of soldiers, tanks, and APCs crossed the area, but there was no one to stop them.

After more than twenty-four hours without food or drink, a disabled Syrian tank stopped next to Amnon, and he was sure

they had discovered him. He left his hiding place and prepared to
surrender. But when the commander of the Syrian tank noticed
him, he was alarmed and raised his hands. Amnon did not know
what to do. He tried to explain to the shocked Syrian that in fact,
Amnon was the one who was the prisoner. In a few seconds the
Syrian got the hint, pulled out his pistol and with a shaking hand
commanded Amnon to follow him. They transferred Amnon to a
nearby Syrian base, where they took his identification and watch.
From this base, they transferred him to Damascus, where he was
imprisoned until his recent release.

THE GENERAL KEPT HIS WORD
by Ilan Kfir
DEFENSE AFFAIRS CORRESPONDENT

On the day the IDF prisoners arrived from Syria, air force commander Major-General Benjamin Peled was among the first to board the Red Cross plane after it landed at Lod Airport. At the plane gate, the commander met a returned prisoner wearing sunglasses. The commander thought the young man was a pilot, and apologized for not recognizing him. But the man, Amnon Sharoni (Sharon) put him at ease. "I'm not a pilot and so you couldn't have known me," he said. At the same time, the returning prisoner asked the air force commander to allow him to fly the country's skies in a Phantom jet.

Much time has passed since that day, and Sharon forgot his request. But Major-General Peled did not forget. Recently, Sharon was surprised to receive an official invitation from the air force to fly in a Phantom. The flight took place last week.

לשכת הרבנות

ג ב ע ת י י ם

רח׳ ויצמן 21
טלפון 722568

ב״ה, יום.....י״ז סיון תשל״ד
7.6.74

כי אעלה ארוכה לך
וממכומיך ארפאך (ירמ׳ ל׳17)

לכבוד
משפ׳ שרון,
קק״ל 3,
ג ב ע ת י י ם

משפחה יקרה!

קבלו נא ברכותינו העמוקות לרגל שוב
אמנון נ"י מן השבי הסורי.

יתן ה׳ לכם בריאות שמחה ונחת רוח שיפצו
אתכם על תקופת הסבל הצער והחרדה ויתקיים בנו כי
אעלה ארוכה לך וממכוחיך ארפאך. נרים כוס ישועה
ופדות.

בברכת שבת שלום
בכבוד ויקר
ובהוקרה כנה,

יוסף גליקסברג
רב העיר

Translation of the Hebrew letter ☞

LETTERS UPON MY RETURN

Office of the Rabbinate
Givatayim
21 Weizmann Street
Telephone: 722568

B″H 17 Sivan 5734
June 7, 1974

For I will restore health unto you,
and I will heal you of your wounds (Jer. 30:17)

TO: The Sharon Family
3 KKL Road
Givatayim

Dear Family,

Please accept our warmest blessings on the occasion of the return of Amnon, may his light shine, from imprisonment in Syria.

May God grant you health and happiness in return for the period of anguish and fear you suffered. May the words of the prophet be fulfilled in you: "For I will restore health unto you, and I will heal you of your wounds." We lift the cup of salvation and liberty.

With blessings for a Shabbat shalom
in sincere appreciation,
Respectfully yours,

Yosef Glicksberg
Municipal Rabbi

143

Givatayim Post Office
Afula Post Office

AF 9306124
Afula 1400 7 16

Mr. Moshe Steinmetz and Family
23 KKL Road
Givatayim

We share in your joy at the return of dear Amnon from captivity.
Velvart Family, Ein-Dor Kibbutz

June 6, 1974
To the Steinmetz Family!
    We share in your happiness with the return of your son Amnon
from captivity.
    The Bonda Family
        Zivah, Ilan, and Zohar

June 6, 1974

Dear Mrs. Steinmetz,
    We have admired your courageous spirit throughout the long
months of anticipation and we share in your happiness.
    Shabbat shalom,
        Hannah Stern and Hannah Sadan

Givatayim Post Office
CHAI 18   7130041
Haifa v 1655 6 13

Moshe Steinmetz
23 KKL Road
Givatayim

We rejoice in your son's return home.
        The Mela Katz Family, Haifa

Givatayim Post Office
Bnei Brak Post Office

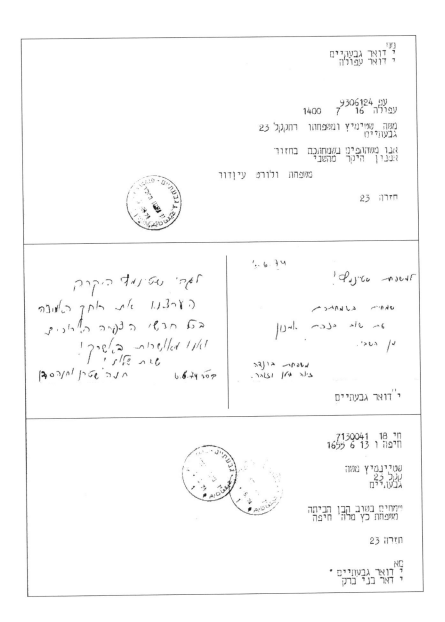

נ.ט.
י דואר גבעתיים
י דואר עפולה

עפ 9306124
עפולה 16 7 1400

משה שפירמיץ ומשפחתו רחנקל 23
גבעתיים

אבן משתופינם בשמחתכם בחזור
ובנין היקר מהשבי

משפחה ולורט עין דור

חזרה 23

6.6.74

ג'דואר גבעתיים

6.6.74

חז 18 7130041
חיפה ו 13 6 1655

שטיינמיץ משה
עגל 23
גבעתיים

יומחיים בשוב הבן הביתה
ומשפחת כץ מרה חיפה

חזרה 23

סא
י דואר גבעתיים •
י דאר בני ברק

🕮 Translation of the Hebrew telegrams

If these photos could only
Convey the power of love
And happiness in which I was welcomed
By my neighbors, acquaintances and a
crowd of anonymous people
Who gathered together to celebrate my return home…

These words
have tried to describe
dark events and places
with all their power.
Now that they have come to an end,
a shining ray of light flickers within me,
purifying this body
that has been forged
with a new soul.

Made in the USA
Middletown, DE
18 March 2024

51710398R00088